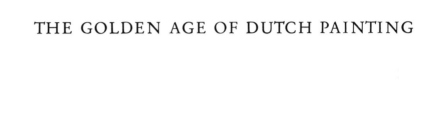

THE GOLDEN AGE OF DUTCH PAINTING

The Golden Age
of Dutch Painting

BARBARA ROSE

FREDERICK A. PRAEGER, Publishers
New York · Washington

BOOKS THAT MATTER

Published in the United States of America in 1969
by Frederick A. Praeger, Inc., Publishers
111 Fourth Avenue, New York, N. Y. 10003

Copyright in Brunswick, West Germany, by Georg Westermann Verlag, Brunswick, 1965

Library of Congress Catalog Card Number: 68–30942

Reproduction, printing, and binding by Georg Westermann, Brunswick, West Germany

CONTENTS

In the Netherlands, the art of painting came to full flower—to its Golden Age—at a time when much of Europe was experiencing the longest wars in its history.

Like the Europeans of the seventeenth century, we are living now in an age of hot and cold war, of civil conflicts and national uprisings; but today, every crisis echoes around the world. In this century, the consequences of a political or social catastrophe are world-wide. In today's world, isolation is impossible.

The world of the seventeenth century seemed larger. Slight distances seemed so great that the Thirty Years' War in Germany had little impact on the business and commerce, science and art of the neighboring Netherlands. On one side of the Rhine, disease and hunger prevailed; on the other, prosperity and order. Here were plundering, murder, and ruin; there, industry, profit, and pleasure.

On a war-torn continent, the little group of independent Dutch states was an oasis of wealth, freedom, and religious toleration. What began as a center of European industry and commerce soon became a cultural center as well. Unfortunately for the Netherlands, when the wars drew to a close and peace returned to Europe, the Dutch lost both cultural and economic leadership.

For nearly a century, Holland was a focus of trade, science, art, and learning, a center of activity so stimulating that the two greatest philosophers of the century, Descartes and Spinoza, both chose to live there—Descartes for a time, and Spinoza throughout his life. The works of art created during this brilliant period provide us with a glowing record of the tastes and customs of the exuberant Dutch people. The Golden Age of Dutch painting coincided with the liberation of the Northern provinces from Spain, and so was born at the same moment as the Dutch nation.

This fortunate time had been preceded by an era of contrasting turmoil for the Netherlands. At the beginning of the seventeenth century, the struggle for independence from Catholic Spain had already occupied the Calvinist provinces of the North for nearly fifty years. The Northern provinces—which eventually made up the Dutch Republic—and the Flemish provinces of the South belonged to Spain in the sixteenth century. They were ruled by Charles V, the most powerful man in Europe. Charles had inherited the Netherlands when his father, Philip the Handsome died in 1506.

By the time he was twenty, Charles ruled all of the Hapsburg lands, which extended from Germany to Spain. In order to keep his vast domain intact, Charles had to spend much of his time at war. He was also obliged to impose stiff taxes on his rich Dutch possessions to support these wars. Of course, the taxes were resented.

Opposition to taxation was nothing, though, compared with the resistance Charles provoked by attempting to suppress Protestantism, which was sweeping like wildfire through Northern Europe. The lessons of the French-Swiss reformer Calvin were especially influential in the Netherlands, where anti-Catholicism only widened the gap between the people and their Spanish rulers. For this reason, we must understand the uprising against the Spaniards as primarily a religious revolution, although there were political and economic issues as well. Religious freedom and independence from Rome were the slogans, but the Dutch were well aware of the economic gains that independence would foster. Finally, it was a social revolution: an uprising of peasants and workers against princes and bishops; a revolt of the landless poor against the Spanish aristocracy who were leeching the country.

Dutch nobles banded together to protect themselves from persecution and to resist the Inquisition, the dread agency that Philip, Charles' son and successor, had exported from Spain for the discovery and punishment of heretics.

Repression and persecution, however, only stimulated the activity of the Calvinists and other reformers. Enthusiasts preached in fields and towns, enflaming the population against the Spaniards and Spanish Catholicism. Rioting spread. During the summer of 1566, furious townspeople and peasants entered the churches of Antwerp and smashed images, altars, pictures, and stained glass. These people were called Iconoclasts, which means image-breakers, because they destroyed the religious images forbidden by the austere Calvinist doctrine. Iconoclasm led to further bloody and bloodless clashes among rival interest groups—Spaniards, Calvinists, peasants, and burghers.

There were consequences for the history of art. No longer would Northern artists paint or carve holy images as they had during the Middle Ages and the Renaissance. The Protestant fear of idolatry, rooted in a strictly literal interpretation of the second commandment ("Thou shalt make no graven image of thy God"), has an interesting parallel in the iconoclastic movement of the early Middle Ages, which banned objects of art from the churches and prohibited artists from treating religious themes. The result in Holland was that the production of religious images virtually ceased. Since few important works of art were created in Holland in the second half of the sixteenth century, it is doubly surprising that this small country, in so short a time, became the center of artistic activity. Astonishingly, the period when the various artistic crafts had lain dormant was followed by the fullest flowering of Dutch art.

One explanation of this flowering is that the long-sought independence from Spain, when it was finally won, called out for expression in new artistic themes. Toward this end, Dutch artists turned to their own lives and landscapes and invented an independent artistic tradition. In the cool, realistic representation of their flat land, spread out under the high, brilliant sky, there was no place for mythological or religious scenes. The life of the village, familiar to all, the refinements of the city, and the beauty of a quiet household were some of the new themes endlessly repeated in new variations. A mule, a tree, or a running brook provided the necessary accents to these peaceful, homely scenes. Finally, there were the people of this new sovereign state. Artists painted peasants and milkmaids, pretty young girls and ugly old crones, resolute businessmen, weary beggars. Pregnant women, children, soldiers, couples, gypsies, Negroes, Jews, fools, scholars, complacent burghers, drinkers, and musicians, depicted without sentimentality, look out from these canvases, as lively as the day they were painted. Still life, too, reached its perfection in seventeenth-century Dutch paintings. Interest was focused on exquisite detail, on things that to other cultures might have seemed trivial and irrelevant. Often, along with a representation of rich possessions, one could find symbolic reference to the Calvinist emphasis on the transitory nature of such earthly goods, no matter how beautiful or enjoyable.

In 1567, the political situation came to a head. William of Orange, the leader of the nobles, fled to Germany, and Philip sent the despotic Duke of Alba to rule the rebellious provinces in the Netherlands. The veteran Spanish general, who was noted for his ruthless cruelty, began immediately to arrest local leaders. Popular nobles like the counts of Egmont and of Hoorn were beheaded at wholesale executions. Many became refugees rather than submit to Alba's tyrannical rule. Of the Dutch nobles, only William of Orange, far away in Germany, was strong enough to mount an attack against Alba. Although he was a Lutheran, William decided to convert and to throw in his lot with the Dutch Calvinists. In 1572, he returned to take up residence in Delft. With the help of the Dutch population, now united under his cause, he was able to drive the Spaniards from the North.

Alba responded by butchering whole townships. The brutal acts of Alba and his troops during the "Spanish Fury" made up one of the darkest pages in European history. For every town that was massacred, however, another held out against the Spaniards.

These events indicate that our impression, derived from the best-known Dutch paintings, of a serene countryside and contented people is only part of the story.

Not so long before Paulus Potter, the popular animal painter, painted his peacefully grazing cows, the Dutch were flooding their own countryside so that provisions could be supplied to besieged cities. Fighting the Spanish along the bloodstained dikes, the Dutch, in desperation, pierced the embankments they had worked so hard to build.

Antwerp eventually fell to the Spaniards; and the Southern provinces were forced to continue under the yoke of Spain. In the North, the Hollanders endured extreme hardship for the sake of future freedom.

As soon as the Northern provinces had freed themselves, workers from the South fled to the North, to escape misery and famine and to enjoy the religious freedom and prosperity of the new republic. Workers in iron, paper, silk, linen, lace, brocade, and tapestry fled the oppressive Spanish rule. The towns of Holland overflowed; Amsterdam grew and prospered as fast as Antwerp shrank. This rapid commercial and industrial growth took place while much of Europe was still at war.

Although the peace that finally ended the bloody war of independence was not signed until 1648, the Northern provinces formed a separate confederation in 1577, called the Union of Utrecht. During the following years, the Dutch confederation gained political order and new allies. But religious questions were still liable to lead to violence, and there was constant quarreling among the various Protestant sects.

Eventually, religious toleration became a law of the state and brought new stability to Holland. Under William's son, the young Prince of Orange, Frederick Henry, who became Stadholder in 1625, the Golden Age of Dutch learning, literature, and painting began. During these years, Holland conquered an eastern empire and gained many possessions in the New World. Wealth and treasure poured in from these colonies, and Holland became one of the richest and most powerful countries in the world, despite its small size. It was as a maritime power, above all, that Holland was supreme. The Dutch were great navigators, equally at home on the oceans and in the network of canals that crisscrossed the flat Dutch countryside. This love of the sea was reflected in the many marine pictures painted by Dutch artists.

Although the seven Northern provinces (Holland, Utrecht, Zeeland, Gelderland, Overijssel, Groningen, and Friesland) had been bound together since 1577, not until the armistice of 1609 did they announce their right to self-determination and religious freedom. As if to celebrate the event, the Dutch nation gave birth to the generation of brilliant painters that included Cuyp, Terborch, Brouwer, Adriaen van Ostade, and the greatest of them all, Rembrandt. After that, each decade until the middle of the century brought forth a new crop of artists: some merely gifted, like Metsu and Teniers; others, like Vermeer, Hals, and Hobbema, painters of consummate genius who joined the highest ranks in the history of art.

The revolution that made the Dutch rich and free had robbed them of the very foundations upon which the other great schools had been built: inherited beliefs, habits, and traditions. There was no longer any need for church pictures and large-scale decorations that were the glory of Flemish art even in the seventeenth century. On the contrary, a nation of practical, hard-headed merchants, bankers, and tradesmen, who valued reality more than mysticism or imagination, demanded an art that was true to nature and the visible world. Not the rewards of heaven or the tortures of hell, but the delights of the here and now—the shimmering silks and rich brocades, the fine glass and silverware, the jewelry and costly laces and embroideries—in short, the excellence of material possessions and the wonders of this world, made tangible by the skill of the artist, were what delighted the taste of men who spent most of their time trading in goods and money. The pleasures of the senses also appealed to these worldly people. Artists painted materials like fur and satin that were soft to the touch; they piled up elaborate arrangements of flowers and good things to eat that spilled forth from the picture like the fruits from a horn of plenty.

This is not to say that the interest in the familiar and the specific lacked universality; on the contrary, a corner of Holland with its canals, forests, and farms might stand for the entire universe. Carefully studied and faithfully recorded, a familiar piece of ground could call forth as profound a response as the grandest religious or mythological scene. This interest in the small, telling detail, an indication of the great curiosity of Dutch painters, was nothing new in Northern artists, who from the very beginning savored the minute ways in which objects differed from one another. In a certain sense, we might see this love of detail, this need to distinguish one glass from another kind, one type of metal from another, one fabric from another, as stemming from the same desire to individualize that made each Dutch portrait not an ideal example of a type but a realistic image of a unique individual.

Free of the stiff, formal Spanish aristocracy, the Dutch encouraged a democratic art that was accessible to the common man, rather than a difficult art full of classical references and complicated hidden meanings. Art flourished in Holland because many people, from the chief of state, the Stadholder, to the humblest peasants, wished to own works of art.

Once the Spaniards were driven out, the seaports of Holland became centers of world trade. After the Spanish economy collapsed as a result of Philip II's wild spending, Amsterdam became the great financial center. Although the nobles had some influence, most of the power in Holland belonged to the "regents," the sturdy, serious burghers we see in the many group portraits painted by such artists as Frans Hals. This was only to be expected, because the revolution that had saved the country and created the republic was a burgher revolution. Through the States General, a body composed of delegates from each provincial assembly, burgher statesmen controlled the country. Political power was mainly in the hands of the mayors and aldermen of the cities, who named each other and were not subject to free elections. The regents—that is, the members of the city councils—naturally were recruited from the nation's most powerful group, the middle class. Most of the population belonged to it, and it ranged from the poorer shop owners to the upper-middle-class regents, who ran the shipping and banking in the country and whose sons and daughters might marry nobility. It is not surprising that nearly all the artists came from the middle class, too.

The Dutch middle class profoundly influenced all of Dutch culture, especially art, which it wished to see created in its own image. Such an influence could be so effective because Dutch art no longer related to the Church. In fact, a church would be the last place in Holland where you would look for a work of art. Just the reverse was true in other parts of Europe, where the Church and the Catholic kings were still the great patrons of art.

Because middle-class householders, unlike the aristocracy and the Church, had no use for large decorations, most Dutch paintings were relatively small. They were at the same time a sign of culture and respectability and a profitable financial investment. Because wealth had increased so rapidly that there was more money than there were ways of spending it, people began putting their extra guilders into paintings, hoping that they would increase in value. For a Dutch peasant or burgher, buying pictures was like buying stocks, as it is for some collectors today.

In this way, the modern art trade came into existence. There was so much buying and selling, not to mention speculation, in paintings, that someone had to act as a middleman between the artist and the public. At first, artists became dealers, acting as agents not only for their own work but for that of their friends as well. David Teniers the Younger and Cornelis de Vos were two well-known artist-dealers. Engravers, especially, since they needed to sell many copies of their mass-produced prints, often became dealers for themselves and others. Jerome de Cock was the most famous of these engraver-dealers. Thus the modern idea of the art market had its origin in seventeenth-century Holland, when artists first began producing their wares for clients they did not know and selling them through middlemen. Previously, most works had been commissioned, that is, ordered to the wishes of the purchaser. But, in seventeenth-century Holland, civic scenes and portraits were almost the only works made to special order. For the most part, Dutch artists, like modern artists, painted what they wished; and like contemporary artists, they were subject to the harsh laws of supply and demand and to the whims of fashion. One year, for example, people might be buying tavern scenes, while the next they liked landscapes. When the public liked landscapes, the painter of tavern scenes would be out of luck. In fact, even Rembrandt fell out of fashion and had his pictures rejected.

Life was difficult for these unfortunate painters who produced works for a fickle market that found no buyers. As long as a work was commissioned in advance, the artist was assured of a sale. But as soon as he began producing for a free market and handing his work over to a middleman, the artist, though he may have gained the freedom to paint what he liked, lost his security. The fierce competition of the art market meant that many artists lived a miserable hand-to-mouth existence. Sometimes it seemed that the greater a painter was, the better were his chances of dying poor. The leading Dutch painters—Rembrandt, Hals, and Vermeer, not to mention Pieter de Hooch and Jacob van Ruisdael—were constantly plagued by financial worries. And Hobbema apparently had to give up painting altogether.

In Holland, collecting paintings was not the right of just a small, privileged class, but an interest of all classes. One writer tells us that in the seventeenth century almost every Dutchman had his own picture gallery.

Among these picture collectors were rich merchants, whose collections covered a wide variety of subjects, envoys from foreign countries, laborers and tradesmen, book dealers, as well as burgomasters and officials. Even peasants, canal boatmen, and shipping agents collected pictures. A contemporary reporter tells us that at a Rotterdam fair in 1641, the buyers were mainly members of the lower middle class and peasants.

This widespread interest in art created a demand so great that there were literally thousands of authentic and would-be artists. In the middle of the century, in Amsterdam alone, there were 300 painters and only 70 butchers. For every baker, there were 2 artists. Imagine the situation if this were the case in New York or London today! But the art boom could not last. After 1620, so many pictures were on the art market in Holland that the supply exceeded the demand, and many artists could not sell their work. The inflation of the art world eventually lowered the level of quality. Often, routine talent replaced creative originality with the spirit of the marketplace. Greed led unscrupulous artists to copy the work of the great masters. The market was flooded with forgeries.

In order to make a living in this highly competitive situation, artists began to restrict themselves to a narrow range of themes. This was a striking change from the Renaissance ideal of the artist as the universal genius who could produce sculpture and architecture, music and poetry. In Holland, even the greatest masters—with the exception of Rembrandt—specialized: Ruisdael, Van Goyen, and Hobbema were landscape painters; Frans Hals was the master of the portrait; De Hooch and Metsu created scenes of interiors; Brouwer and Steen painted the plain peasant milieu; Kalf and Heda were leaders in the field of still life. But specialization went even further. In landscape painting, for example, there were specialists in seascapes (so-called "marines"), winter landscapes, and night landscapes ("nocturnes"). De Witte was a well-known specialist in architectural painting, and Terborch was known primarily for his ability to paint fine materials.

Only Rembrandt refused to be confined in a narrow range. Portraitist and landscape painter, he painted magnificent still lifes, Biblical scenes, and genre pictures as well. Rembrandt was the great solitary figure who towered over his contemporaries. An outsider, he seldom achieved the economic success of many colleagues who were less gifted artists but better businessmen. Although he produced about 700 paintings, 300 etchings, and more than 1,000 drawings, he died penniless and in debt; the personal estate of the greatest Dutch painter was described as "a few articles of clothing, linens, and diverse work tools."

FORERUNNERS

Pieter Bruegel, *Self-portrait* (drawing)

To locate the beginnings of Dutch art, we must go back to the art of Flanders in the early fifteenth century. During the transition from the Middle Ages to the Renaissance, painters like the brothers Hubert and Jan van Eyck, Rogier van der Weyden, and his teacher Robert Campin, known as the Master of Flémalle, made the Netherlands a focus of artistic activity, second only to Italy. To these early Netherlandish painters, whom art historians call "primitives," we can trace the foundation of the Dutch as well as the Flemish schools of painting.

The specialty of the Netherlandish primitives was a cool, unsentimental realism. This fidelity to nature was especially suited to portraiture, a field in which they excelled. Here in the North, painters could develop these qualities in a way that Italian painters, who were the direct heirs of the highly formal antique tradition and the stylized, unrealistic Byzantine tradition, could not. Eventually, realism came to Italy through the influence of the Netherlandish masters who traveled there during the fifteenth century. By the end of the fifteenth century, however, the situation was reversed. The attraction of Italian art was so strong that the Northerners surrendered, almost to a man. In the early fifteenth century, the town of Bruges in Flanders had been a place of pilgrimage for artists. A hundred years later, they visited the city only to copy Raphael's tapestry cartoons being woven there for the Vatican.

By 1500, instead of visiting Bruges or Ghent, Northern artists chose to go South for the *Wanderjahr*—the term for the year of travel that traditionally followed a young artist's apprenticeship. Two of these were Jan Gossaert (called Mabuse after his birthplace), who went to Rome in 1508, and Jan van Scorel, who was described in 1524 as a "follower of Raphael." At home in the Netherlands, painters joined the ranks of the "Romanists," as those who imitated Raphael and Michelangelo were styled. Among the Romanists were painters like Gossaert and Van Scorel, as well as Quentin Massys and, later, Frans Floris and Marten de Vos. These Romanists tried to combine the pictorial simplicity of early Netherlandish painting with the architectural compositions of the Italian Renaissance, which seemed more heroic and monumental.

Despite the extent to which the Northerners copied the Italians, the robust, realistic spirit of earlier Netherlandish painting was not totally renounced. Some remained almost entirely free of Italian influences. The most important of these painters who remained true to the native tradi-

Pieter Bruegel, *Landscape with St. Jerome* (drawing)

tion was Pieter Bruegel. Although he, too, traveled in Italy, one finds almost no sign of contact with the Italian Renaissance in his work. Indeed, his work stands in clear opposition to the taste of the times; and for this reason it represents the most significant link between the Netherlandish painters of the fifteenth century and those of the Golden Age of Dutch painting.

In Bruegel's work, we find the origin of many themes that became popular in the seventeenth century. In his many paintings of peasants and laborers, Bruegel illustrated the everyday life of the common man. In the seventeenth century, genre painters like Jan Steen and Adriaen Brouwer would be inspired by Bruegel's peasant feasts and dances. The rough, coarse villagers of Bruegel's *Peasant Dance* (p. 17), for example, look like the cousins of Brouwer's *Card-Playing Peasants in the Tavern* (p. 100). However, the moral lessons suggested by Bruegel's paintings are not found in the seventeenth-century genre scenes. The latter were meant only to show simple people enjoying themselves.

Besides his genre scenes, Bruegel's naturalistic Northern landscapes, which were free of any Italianate tendency to idealize, were an important source for the development of an independent landscape tradition in the coming centuries. Bruegel was among the first to reveal the special charms of the native landscape. He also studied the changing seasons in a way that inspired future Dutch painters. In his paintings of the months of the year (pp. 18 and 19), landscape is always seen in relationship to human activity. Bruegel's vision is expressed in hard outlines and strong, unbroken local colors. He never developed the eye for flickering atmosphere and radiant light reflections that would be the speciality of his seventeenth-century Dutch heirs.

Even after Bruegel, a few retained independence of the fashionable Italian influence. In the late sixteenth century, however, most landscape painters ignored the rustic native landscape in favor of an imaginary idealized scene. For this reason, the landscape tradition in the North began to lose its early strength. In Italy, the sixteenth-century style called Mannerism was a continuation of the Renaissance. In the North, the comparable style was contrived and sweet, leaning heavily on Italian examples. Mannerism was finally ended in Italy with the fresh vitality of painters like the Carracci and Caravaggio, whose simple, direct expressiveness and dramatic play of light and shadow became the model for many Northern artists.

Although Caravaggio had no pupils, he was the decisive influence on the generation of painters that included Rembrandt. One of the most important painters to fall under his sway was the young Dutch painter Hendrick Terbrugghen of Utrecht. The young Terbrugghen had arrived in Rome in 1604, while Caravaggio was still working there. He seems to have fallen in with a group of Northern genre painters, known as "Kleinmeister" or "little masters" because of the small scale of their works. They had come to study Italian painting and lived together in a bohemian neighborhood of their own. We know very little about Terbrug-

Pieter Bruegel, *Peasant Dance*, p. 17

Adriaen Brouwer, *Card-Playing Peasants in the Tavern*, p. 100

Pieter Bruegel, *Return of the Hunter: Month of January*, p. 18

Pieter Bruegel, *Harvest: Month of June*, p. 19

Pieter Bruegel, *Peasant Dance* (detail)

Pieter Bruegel, *Harvest: Month of June* (detail)

Joos de Momper, *Autumn* (detail)

Abraham Bloemaert, *Shepherd under a Withered Tree* (drawing)

ghen's early years. Although he imitated Caravaggio, we do not know whether he was personally acquainted with the hot-blooded Italian who revolutionized painting. We do know, however, that Terbrugghen joined the Utrecht painters' guild after his return from Italy.

In Utrecht, the hard, sculptural realism, dramatic lighting, and half-length figures of beggars and gypsies, enlarged as if seen very close up, which Terbrugghen had borrowed from Caravaggio, soon found an audience. Bold and striking, these paintings quickly set a vogue in the North for such sensational pictures. In Terbrugghen's energetic Caravaggesque style seen in *The Flute Player* (p. 84), there was something new, dynamic, and lively—a drama, monumentality, and psychological expressiveness—that could be translated into the newly aggressive voice of Dutch national feeling. Soon there was a whole group of painters who eagerly took over Terbrugghen's imported style. One of them was the light-hearted Utrecht painter Gerard van Honthorst, who was known in Italy as "Gerardo della Notte" (Gerard of the Night) because he painted so many night scenes and candlelit scenes. The daring art of the Utrecht Caravaggists, Terbrugghen, Honthorst, and Dirck van Baburen, signals the opening of Holland's Golden Age of painting. In a now independent Holland, their fresh new art meant a denial of the religious themes and thought of the Middle Ages, a rejection of the spirit of the Catholic Counter-Reformation, and a repudiation of Spain and absolutism. It developed out of a rich and fruitful intermingling of native and Italian elements, on which Dutch painters were able at last to build a great independent tradition.

Hendrick Terbrugghen, *The Flute Player*, p. 84

LANDSCAPE

A small strip of flat land under an open sky that fills three-quarters of the picture; a silvery horizon, vague and misty where earth and sky meet; clear, glittering atmosphere that hints of the sea—that is the Dutch landscape. Anyone who has been to Holland will recognize it in the paintings of the Dutch masters.

But even people who have not seen Holland with their own eyes can still see it through those of the great seventeenth-century Dutch landscape painters, so little has modern civilization changed the original appearance of its windmills, dikes, canals, and scattered villages. Indeed, no literary description, no color photograph, no matter how perfect, could capture its magical light and austere mood better than the paintings of the Dutch masters. After them, only the French Impressionists could keep landscapes so free of implied symbols and be so content to depict it simply as itself, for its own sake.

The Dutch masters, however, were not yet "plein-air" or outdoors naturalists like the French. They did not paint outside, as would the Impressionists of the nineteenth century. Their landscapes, which seem so faith-

Aelbert Cuyp, *Landscape with Cows* (drawing)

ful to nature, were actually painted indoors. The result of many trips to the country, they were composed in the studio from the fresh, quick drawings and sketches made by all the great artists of the time. For these men, the artistic process was a product not only of vision but of memory. Their landscapes are silent and contemplative, reflecting tranquil thought, as well as deep love for the simple and true, and joy in the visible world. The development of Dutch painting is characterized by close ties between drawing and landscape painting. When the Dutch painter went out to study nature, he took a pencil or pen, rather than a brush. The draftsman isolates branches and twigs, since everything has interest for him not from the point of view of color or tone, but from the point of view of line. The first seventeenth-century Dutch landscapes, those of Esaias van de Velde and Willem Buytewech, resemble drawings in paint.

Landscape had always played an important role in Netherlandish painting. Even in the fifteenth century, before landscape painting had become an independent speciality, Jan van Eyck had set the Paradise scene of his famous Ghent altarpiece against a broad, rolling landscape. The silvery vapors swimming in the distant background of the Ghent altarpiece were echoed again and again in the wide horizons and open seas of later seventeenth-century landscapes. But in the Ghent altarpiece, the figures in the foreground are still dominant. Landscape has to be glimpsed over their heads. In order to paint mountains with the greatest sense of distance and grandeur, the primitives were forced to exercise more than one viewpoint: a bird's-eye view of the landscape and a head-on view from ground level for the figures in the foreground, so that they would not appear distorted. By the end of the sixteenth century, however, artists had learned to combine these two ways of seeing.

A high horizon and more than one viewpoint are signs of primitive paintings. In many fifteenth-century paintings, water runs from the bottom of the picture up to the high horizon. Soon Flemish painters like Joachim Patinir found that an impression of distance could be achieved by making remote objects smaller and distant colors hazier. By using a cool, blue-green tonality in the background, painters found that they were able to intensify this impression of distance, because it is a property of cool colors to seem to recede before the eye. The separation of landscape into three distinct zones (foreground, middle ground, and background), each dominated by a different color, became a convention of Netherlandish painting. It was abandoned only in the seventeenth century, when painters learned to unify space and make it appear continuous by the use of light. Other devices, too, were invented in order to ensure the continuity of space. Details were subordinated and related to the whole, compositions were adapted in which strong diagonals led the eye from the foreground directly into the background.

According to Max J. Friedländer, an eminent writer on the subject, fifteenth-century Netherlandish landscapes are merely geographical ground plans. The continuous space of seventeenth-century landscapes, on the other hand, resembles "a river without banks, and the things in it

Joos de Momper, *Inlet on the Gebirge* (drawing)

resemble the waves." In the beginning, Netherlandish landscape was merely the piling up of many details; in its final development—in the work of Rembrandt, Ruisdael, and Hobbema—it became a single unified vision from a consistent single point of view.

Other early masters besides the Flemish Van Eyck and Rogier van der Weyden and the Dutchman, Albert van Ouwater, gave glimpses in the backgrounds of their religious paintings of broad landscape with running water and silhouettes of towns with rays of light streaming into them. The problem of deep space, which the Italians had approached through linear perspective, was solved in their work through aerial or atmospheric perspective. This method was refined by sixteenth-century artists like Patinir, one of the first artists to specialize exclusively in landscape.

Dirck Bouts was among the earliest painters to follow Van Eyck in his discovery of landscape. Of Bouts, Friedländer writes, "Delightedly he crowds the pictorial wealth of vegetable forms into the narrow compass of the picture. He lights up the painting as a whole according to the position of the sun and the formation of the clouds; he observes reflections as well as cast shadows." Another Dutchman, who is often called the founder of the Dutch school, the Haarlem master Geertgen tot Sint Jans, who was active around 1480, also contributed to the development of landscape painting. For example, he set his famous *Saint John the Baptist* in a rich landscape. Deep in contemplation, the melancholy seated

Geertgen tot Sint Jans,
Saint John the Baptist

24

figure of the Baptist is contrasted with the natural peace and harmony that surrounds him. Like later Dutch masters, Geertgen relates man to nature in mood and expression.

Light and atmosphere provided an essential element in the Netherlandish tradition from its beginnings. Even in the sixteenth century, when the Italian influence countered the Northern tradition of realism, the Dutch sense for an airy, light-filled landscape remained unaffected. It was still in such a luminous setting that Pieter Bruegel painted his parables, children's games, and peasant feasts. The Romanists, too, set their rich narratives and allegories against such characteristic Netherlandish landscapes. In Italy, the Venetians, and especially Caravaggio, emphasized light as a pictorial element. In Holland, on the other hand, the use of light to model and to suggest space was not an innovation but a rediscovery. Whether the impulse came from Italy and Caravaggio or directly from the native tradition is not important. What matters is the extent to which painters in the North became interested in light in the seventeenth century. We may note, however, that this new interest in light was roughly contemporary with the new interest of philosophy and science in visible nature. At the same time that the Dutch painters were experimenting

Hercules Seghers, *Rocky Landscape* (etching)

with the appearance of light, scientists like Newton were discussing the physical make-up of light, and Dutch scientists were experimenting with optics, the science of light.

Although certain elements of the new atmosperic landscape were traditional in Holland, there was a change of emphasis after 1620. We can observe this in comparing *Autumn* by Joos de Momper (p. 20), painted around the turn of the century, with a landscape by his younger contemporary, Hercules Seghers (p. 32), dated 1620. An example of the older tradition, Momper's landscape is full of fine detail and diverting episodes. The more modern Seghers, on the other hand, is no longer involved with such busy activity. His few small figures tell no story; they serve merely to intensify the feeling of deep space. For this reason, they are small in relation to the forms in the foreground, as we expect distant figures to be. Seghers' picture is no longer just a sum of its details. It is understandable only as a whole—a broad, peaceful landscape, dramatically illuminated by the sinking sun, undisturbed by human activity.

Not more than twenty years lie between these two paintings. Yet the whole conception of the world has changed. Of course, Seghers was advanced for his time. He was a unique figure among the earliest painters of Dutch landscape. His work had a decisive influence on the future of

Joos de Momper, *Autumn*, p. 20
Hercules Seghers, *Landscape*, p. 32

Jan van Goyen, *Landscape with Ferry Boat* (drawing)

Jacob van Ruisdael, *Peasant Cottages* (drawing)

landscape painting. Rembrandt, for example, although he was not a pupil of Seghers, was among the first to learn from his exciting interpretation of nature. Seghers is in many ways a fascinating artist. A morbid, eccentric personality, he has challenged psychologists with his fanatical images of a wild, pathless nature described by a tangled net of lines. The over-agitated character of his nervous line is even more evident in his graphic work (p. 25). Seghers' fantastic landscapes are filled with mountain ranges pitted with craters, ruins, and distant stony wastelands. They are bathed in a cold, mysterious light and peopled by nightmarish demons. In the work of modern artists like the Expressionists and the Surrealists, we find images from a similarly anxious world. They have rediscovered a world that Seghers was exploring in the seventeenth century.

Hercules Seghers, *Rocky Landscape*, p. 25

Seghers suggests an untamed nature full of unknown forces and unseen dangers. The peaks and passes of Bruegel's paintings of the Alps (p. 18), the most obvious residue of his trip to Italy, were a source for Seghers. After Seghers, nature was seen as mild and benevolent, reflecting man's new understanding and mastery of the forces of nature. In fact, it was as if men could not enjoy nature until they saw it domesticated in a painting. In a painting, nature seemed less strange and threatening.

Momper, who was a prolific landscape painter, is Bruegel's heir in the boldness of his conception and execution, although he lacks Bruegel's profundity and genius. Gillis van Coninxloo was another painter who learned an important lesson from Bruegel. In 1585, Coninxloo left his native Antwerp to found a colony of painters in Frankenthal, Germany. Ten years later, when he moved to Amsterdam, he became one of the channels of the Flemish landscape tradition for Dutch painters. Meanwhile, in Rome, Adam Elsheimer, a German painter impressed by the lush forests of the Frankenthal school, employed dramatic lighting in a way that soon gained favor with the Dutch.

The typical landscape of Coninxloo and the Frankenthal school is arranged in layers, parallel to the picture surface, like theatrical flats. The sides of the painting are emphasized by dark, massive trees that frame the composition. This type of landscape, in which the spectator feels securely enclosed within a forest sanctuary, differs greatly from the bird's-eye views of the early sixteenth century. Taste for a more intimate type of landscape reflected man's warmer feelings toward nature, which now seemed friendlier, more familiar, and less ominous. In this new type of landscape, trees took up more and more space, their leaves blotting out the sun with dense foliage.

These leafy woods began to resemble a forest wall or a curtain of foliage, dense as a tapestry of leaves. Typical of Coninxloo and the Frankenthal school was a composition with small openings or pathways cut into the wall to let the sun shine through. Coninxloo developed a mechanical way of painting foliage, so that while each leaf was carefully rendered, it was almost identical to all the other leaves. In the paintings of the great seventeenth-century masters, on the other hand, leaves are seen in less detail, but with more variety of shape and color. This tendency to individualize natural forms may be an outcome of newly awakened scientific curiosity. The seventeenth century was the great age of botany as well as physics. It was during the seventeenth century that scientists like Christian Huygens were examining and classifying nature. Coninxloo's rich forests seem damp and lush. The remote landscape of Bruegel and Patinir has become more cozy. We feel comforted by the familiar rather than awed by the strange. Of Coninxloo's great influence in Holland around the turn of the seventeenth century, Karel van Mander, the contemporary chronicler, wrote, "I know of no better landscapist today and observe also that his art is beginning to find very many followers in Holland, and the trees, which stood rather thinly hereabouts, are now beginning to grow like his, though some of their planters might be unwilling to admit this!"

Very different from Coninxloo's dense, fertile groves was the calm, open landscape of Jan van Goyen, who was born in Leyden in 1596. No one loved the typical Dutch landscape so much as he. In many ways a child of the previous century, Van Goyen reveals in his early work how tied he was still to the earlier tradition. His teacher, Esaias van de Velde, was

Salomon van Ruysdael, *River Landscape*

Jan van Goyen, *Village Church Amidst Dunes*

Aert van der Neer, *Winter Landscape*

Hercules Seghers, *Landscape*

one of a group of painters whose landscapes were filled with lively figures in the manner of Bruegel and Momper. At first, Van Goyen, too, created small, carefully constructed paintings, crowded with lovingly executed details—people, houses, trees, carts—in tangled profusion. But sometime around 1630, the year of Van de Velde's death, Van Goyen changed his style. His paintings took on a new simplicity. His brilliant, strong browns, greens, blues, and reds were dimmed and blended into an atmospheric haze through the use of broken tones. The horizon line, which had run through the middle of his early paintings, sank to make a painting three-quarters sky—a previously unknown prominence. Before this, only Seghers' work had given the spectator such a viewpoint and so deep a distance.

Van Goyen worked quickly, easily, and steadily. His paintings were pleasing and easy to understand. They were also easy to imitate. Characteristically, he presents a view as if from below. The horizon is near the bottom margin of the picture. The foreground is a dark strip that makes distances seem more luminous and airy by contrast. Brownish, yellowish, and greenish tones merge into one another, rather than being graded like the zones in a Patinir landscape. The relationship of figures to landscape has changed; figures are now accessories to sky and water. Van Goyen likes gray days. His is a landscape of poetic melancholy. Not only the air but objects themselves are rendered weightless and colorless, almost as immaterial as the veils of atmosphere. Land is seen as a triangle lying on its side, which rises from the bottom of the picture. Earth runs like a wedge into the distance, heightening the sense of deep space. And all this is described with fluid, loose brushstrokes.

In Van Goyen's mature work the zone of the sky expresses the mood of the painting. Filled with diffuse clouds and atmospheric mist through which light filters, it bathes the whole landscape with its brilliance. In these late Van Goyen landscapes, color is only a muted echo of the dazzling sky above. In a painting like *Landscape with Two Oaks* (p. 40), we see that the influence of light on color, which the Impressionists were the first to understand fully, is already an important element. Clouds here have a variety of densities. In the background, they are vaporous and drifting; in the middle ground, dark and heavy with rain; in the foreground, light filters through to illuminate the scene below.

Corresponding to the various intensities of light are the intensities of color. In the background, we see streaks of blue against a paler blue; in the shadowed foreground, a greenish brown and a cold grayish white where the rays of the sun break through the gathering thunderstorm. Pure green has no place in this twilight; it is present only in mixtures with blue, brown, and gray. In fact, only one color is seen full strength: the red jacket of the peasant who occupies the picture's midpoint. Because it also cuts the horizon line, this figure is the optical and compositional focus of the painting. Not even the massive gnarled trees that dominate the picture with their size can upset the harmonious balance of space and color thus achieved.

Jan van Goyen, *Landscape with Two Oaks*, p. 40

33

Salomon van Ruysdael, *Fishing Boats* (drawing)

Jan van Goyen,
*Village Church Amidst
Dunes*, p. 30

Van Goyen's *Village Church Amidst Dunes* (p. 30), reveals an even more dynamic sense of balance. Here the horizon line cuts diagonally through the dunes. This exciting movement is balanced by the vertical form of the church, looking upright and stable. This type of composition permitted Van Goyen to create a dynamic spatial order, which complemented the liveliness of the sky with its constantly changing light. In a late work like the *Landscape with Two Oaks*, he exchanged this dramatic tension for a majestic stillness, in which movement has ceased and is replaced by an abiding calm. The most sensitive and lyrical landscape painter of his time, Van Goyen eliminated all symbolic overtones from landscape. Through a masterful handling of colors and development of painting technique, he arrived at a formal simplicity that accurately expressed the spirit of his native countryside.

In the work of Jacob van Ruisdael, born in Haarlem in 1628, landscape became more dramatic than it had been in Van Goyen's quiet works. Ruisdael, too, allowed the sky to occupy a large area of the painting and gave it a dominant role. Flooding the picture with atmospheric light, he made the flat land of his small native country seem quite heroic. But Ruisdael was not drawn to the broad, panoramic view of Van Goyen.

34

He was more interested in the structure and balance of large masses and dramatic contrasts of light and dark. In his *Mill on the Wijk* (p. 41), Ruisdael has made his illusion of reality so convincing that you can almost feel the wind rippling the water, filling the windmill's sail, moving the reeds, and blowing the clouds. The dazzling sunlight, which casts heavy shadows, also illuminates colors with a brilliant intensity. The composition is as striking as the use of light. The horizon line is not level; it runs obliquely through trees, houses, and dunes to join the coastline at a sharp angle. Exciting diagonals and oblique lines form a triangle with the framing edge of the picture. Another triangle is formed by the water in the foreground as it pushes against the land, setting up a double movement of land pressing against water, and water pressing against land. The result, despite so much tension, conveys surprising peace and calm.

Jacob van Ruisdael had learned the principles of his art from his uncle, the famous Haarlem landscape painter, Salomon van Ruysdael. Jacob was a moody personality, subject to fits of melancholy and depression. His art, with its picturesque ruins and graveyards, was especially appreciated by the Romantic poets and painters of the nineteenth century. In fact, the great Goethe praised Ruisdael for the poetry of his vision.

Jacob van Ruisdael loved the strange and exotic. The theme of the demonic in nature is one that appealed to him as a young man. A trip to

Jacob van Ruisdael, *Mill on the Wijk,* p. 41

Philips Koninck, *Landscape*

Germany allowed him to see the work of the early German landscape painters, especially Elsheimer, who established contact between Italian and Northern landscape art. On this trip, Ruisdael learned to appreciate the beauty of wild, deserted mountain forests, with their rushing rivers and plummeting waterfalls. He recorded these impressions in paintings that reflect nothing of his quiet homeland. In these early works, Ruisdael painted the tragic aspect of nature: forests of dying oak deserted in winter; stagnant water choked with plants and algae. These dead things, like the decaying ruins he also loved to paint, suggest the transitory nature of life and of beauty. This theme of mortality is a favorite of seventeenth-century painters. We will find it again when we study the Vanitas type of still life.

Jacob van Ruisdael loved the sense of solitude and peace he discovered alone with nature. Therefore, he eliminated human figures from such masterpieces as the *Forest Lake* and the two *Jewish Graveyards*. The work of his uncle, Salomon van Ruysdael, on the other hand, reveals none of this melancholy. In Salomon's pictures, nature is seen as the

Hendrick Avercamp, *Winter Sports on the Ice* (drawing)

Philips Koninck, *View over a River Landscape*

Jacob van Ruisdael, *The Water Mill*

Right: Paulus Potter, *Out to Pasture*

Jan van Goyen, *Landscape with Two Oaks*

On the following pages:

Aelbert Cuyp, *River Landscape*
Isaac van Ostade, *A Frozen Canal*

Jacob van Ruisdael, *Mill on the Wijk*

Meindert Hobbema, *Avenue in Middelharnis*

fitting counterpart of man, the power that links Creator and created. Water is not the antagonist of land, but its companion. In Salomon van Ruisdael's sunny landscapes, there is no message. Craftmanship and the decorative are important in themselves.

In his *River Landscape* (p. 29), Salomon van Ruysdael combines water and air in a pearly unity. Land remains outside the picture—a cut-off tree on the left indicating that the picture continues beyond its boundaries. This type of composition, which seems to overflow beyond its frame, is typical of Baroque painting. Serving to suggest deep space, the little sailboats in the background float off into an unknown distance. Everything in this painting is pulled together and used to give the impression of deep space. For example, the dark in the foreground leads us back to the little sticks in the water and the one lone bird in the distance. The bright air shimmers through the transparent darkness. In the finest sense, Salomon van Ruysdael's landscapes are related to those of Van Goyen, even though they never achieve the latter's greatness.

Salomon van Ruysdael, *River Landscape*, p. 29

One of the foremost Dutch landscape painters was Philips Koninck of Amsterdam, who brought the art to a new height. He, too, ignored anecdotal details in favor of general effect. He understood how to represent the calm beauty of the flat countryside with cool objectivity. His compositions, such as *View over a River Landscape* (p. 37), seem quite simple to us. Usually, the viewer finds himself looking down from a high point of view on a panoramic landscape. From this high viewpoint, the horizon line appears to run roughly through the middle of the painting. In Koninck's work, land and sky remain clearly separated; and there is no fuzziness at the horizon. He achieves a great sense of depth through his arrangement of the various landscape elements. Often, there are stones, earth, and bushes in the foreground; sometimes a small tree or two. Behind these, long rows of trees and bushes and then more trees are arranged in small strips often parallel with the picture's edge. Then behind them, there is often a running stream, an orchard, a road, fields, trees, and so on up to the horizon. Although the general tone is a brownish green, colors are painted more or less as they appear in nature. The influence of Seghers and Rembrandt can be remarked in his work, but Koninck dismisses from his landscapes any fantastic or demonic element.

Philips Koninck, *View over a River Landscape*, p. 37

Like Koninck, Meindert Hobbema was a great realist. The pupil of Jacob van Ruisdael, he was considered Ruisdael's heir as the leading Amsterdam landscape painter. But Hobbema's temperament was quite different from Ruisdael's. He is more sensual, less spiritual and poetic, a difference that is perhaps reflected in his choice of more vivid colors. The tragic mood of Ruisdael, the lyric melancholy of Van Goyen, and even the ascetic strength of Koninck are missing from Hobbema's more conventional landscapes, which tend to remain more purely formal arrangements. Hobbema's circle of themes was narrow; he made numerous variations on groups of trees, mills, picturesque ruins, and peasant houses. Usually his landscapes were peopled with many figures and animals. But despite

Jan Porcellis, *Marine* (drawing)

Meindert Hobbema,
*Avenue in Middel-
harnis*, p. 44

these limitations, he treated his few themes with a lively freshness. His most important work, the *Avenue in Middelharnis* (p. 44), is a powerful painting that replaces the idyllic with a certain harshness. The sharply foreshortened road takes one rapidly back into space. The many horizontal and vertical axes create a vigorous tension that results not from emotional content but from purely compositional stresses. In Hobbema's work, there is no unnecessary sentiment, no softened line, and no sliding scale of colors. On the contrary, his objective nature prefers the sober light and clear, transparent air of midday. In the spontaneous, free execution of this masterpiece, Hobbema was far ahead of his time. After his death, he quickly fell into obscurity, to be rediscovered only in the nineteenth century by the Barbizon painters and the Impressionists Sisley and Pisarro.

In the seventeenth century, when landscape was a special theme dominating the lifework of certain artists, the field of landscape was even further subdivided. Landscape painters became specialists in scenes of winter, of night, of the sea, and so forth. The great master of the winter landscape was Hendrick Avercamp, who was born in Amsterdam in 1585. Stylistically, Avercamp belongs to the new period of landscape painting, although his densely populated panoramic scenes are related to those of Pieter Bruegel, the original creator of the winter landscape. But Avercamp goes beyond Bruegel in his realistic treatment of the season. For example, in his *Return of the Hunter* (p. 18), Bruegel creates a rich fantasy of peasant life. In Avercamp's work (p. 36), on the other hand,

Pieter Bruegel,
*Return of the Hunter:
Month of January,*
p. 18
Hendrick Avercamp,
*Winter Sports
on the Ice*, p. 36

we have the true Dutch landscape with its high sky, typical peasant houses, windmills, and cool, silvery atmosphere.

Barely twenty years younger than Avercamp, Aert van der Neer shows still further development in the tradition of the winter landscape. In his landscapes, such as *Winter Landscape* (p. 31), there are many figures, but Van der Neer no longer strews them across the face of the landscape as Avercamp did. He binds them in groups, leaving areas between groups through which we can glimpse deep space. Van der Neer was always more interested in the content of a work than in its subject. He could transform a village romp into a fantastic vision by the mysterious cold light of the moon shining through thick clouds. Moonlight allowed him to create a whole new scale of color values. Its irridescent reflections on water and ice and the dramatic silhouettes it created all expressed the poetry in Van der Neer's view of nature. Like Jacob van Ruisdael, Van der Neer was appreciated by the German romantic painters, who saw him as one of their own forerunners.

The discovery of the sea and the new importance of Amsterdam as a trading center led to the development of the Dutch marine pictures that celebrated Holland's great trading vessels and battleships. Because Hol-

Aert van der Neer,
Winter Landscape,
p. 31

Willem van de Velde
the Younger, *Ships* (drawing)

land was dependent on the sea, for both defense and trade, everything that had to do with sea travel was important to her people. It is not surprising that painters adopted this theme and found a ready market for pictures of ships at sea, beset by storm, or at rest in the harbor.

The development of marine painting had two phases. The first, which we might call "fantastic," began in the sixteenth century, with Bruegel's representations of ships. These early marine paintings stressed the drama and adventure of sailing. The plight of men threatened by wind and wave, helpless before all-powerful nature, was the theme of this period. The Flemish painter Andries van Eertvelt, for example, painted such fantastic paintings (p. 49), of ships tossed like paper boats in the dark, churning waves.

Andries van Eertvelt, *Stormy Sea*, p. 49

The second phase of marine painting was more factual; the sea voyage became a symbol of national expansion, no longer an object of fantasy. One of the first painters to depict the sea this way was Jan Porcellis, who had an important role in Van Goyen's artistic development. In his marine drawing (p. 46), the ship plays only a minor role. Porcellis concentrates instead on the motion of the waves, the light, and the changing reflections on the water.

Jan Porcellis, *Marine*, p. 46

Marine painting developed relatively late. Its most fruitful phase began at about 1650, when painters were acquiring new knowledge of nautical affairs and increased technical facility. The most important of the new group of marine painters was Willem van de Velde the Younger. From his father, a nautical draftsman in Amsterdam, the young Willem acquired an interest in ship's voyages as well as a practical knowledge of their construction and operation. Van de Velde was a pupil of Simon de Vlieger, at that time an unchallenged master of the sea piece, who taught him tonal painting and nautical drawing. It is hard to know which to admire more in Van de Velde's paintings—the brilliant tones of light, water, clouds, and atmosphere, or his accurate knowledge of ship construction and sailing. Van de Velde loved water that was still or scarcely moving, and the bright reflections under the harbor piers. His best picture is probably *The Cannon Volley* (p. 52). Although the subject is a battle weapon, we feel that its salute has a peaceful meaning. The mildness of the blue sky and gentle fluttering of the sails suggest that the sound, if we could hear it, might disturb the silence but not the tranquillity of this scene.

Willem van de Velde the Younger, *The Cannon Volley*, p. 52

Among the important marine painters of the mid-century was Reinier Nooms, who was known as "Zeeman," or "seaman," because he painted so many pictures of the sea. Nooms never tired of painting the sea around Amsterdam, with its familiar shoreline, or the busy harbor with ships lying at anchor (p. 51), or slipping out to sea.

Another special group of mid-century landscapists were the colonial painters. They were stimulated to paint foreign scenes by the rise of Hol-

Reinier (Zeeman) Nooms, *Ships at Anchor off Amsterdam*, p. 51

Andries van Eertvelt, *Stormy Sea* (detail)

50   Frans Post, *Brazilian Landscape*

Reinier (Zeeman) Nooms, *Ships at Anchor off Amsterdam* 51

52   Willem van de Velde the Younger, *The Cannon Volley*

land as a colonial power. In 1602, a Dutch East India Company had been founded that extended from Batavia over much of Indonesia, and began to monopolize South East Asian commerce. In 1626, the Dutch bought Manhattan Island for the legendary bargain price of $24.00. In 1652, they founded the colony of Kaapstadt, later Capetown, and in 1667, they claimed part of South America. Among the weatherbeaten adventurers who explored this unknown territory were a number of artists who could not make a living at home and hoped to find their fortune in the colonies. Once abroad, they continued to paint, combining their impressions of the exotic Dutch empire with memories of their native landscapes.

The best known of these colonial painters was Frans Post, who was born in Leyden in 1612. Post followed Prince Johann Moritz van Nassau to Brazil in 1637. He remained there for seven years, painting the strange jungle landscape with its tropical vegetation and dark natives. His genuine feeling for the typical Brazilian folklore, and his treatment of these primitive themes (p. 50) recalls nineteenth-century master Henri Rousseau's paintings of the tropics. After his return to Holland, Post continued to paint such bizarre themes from either sketches or memory.

Frans Post, *Brazilian Landscape*, p. 50

The specialty of Post's contemporary Paulus Potter was quite different from the exotic Brazilian landscape. Potter chose to paint the familiar Dutch meadows: the pastures, shrubs, solitary trees, flowers, water plants, and, above all, the horned cattle who grazed there (p. 39). Although these lumbering beasts might seem a doubtful attraction, Potter's fame was so great that he had a whole circle of followers and imitators. Potter did not idealize the stupid expressions of the grazing cows. He concentrated instead on representing their powerful bodies and the spacious summer scene with a true feeling for the simple life of the land.

Paulus Potter, *Out to Pasture*, p. 39

Finally, we come to four related landscape painters who were born in the first quarter of the seventeenth century. Isaac van Ostade, born in Haarlem in 1621, painted more subtle although less powerful paintings than his older brother, the genre painter Adriaen van Ostade. Isaac's most important works were winter landscapes, such as *A Frozen Canal* (p. 43). His contemporary, Nicolaes Berchem, was also a native of Haarlem. Berchem's landscapes (pp. 59, 74), with their mild Southern light filtered through an Italianate landscape, were very popular and influenced many of his followers. Like Berchem, Aelbert Cuyp of Dordrecht (pp. 22, 42) was drawn to clear, brilliant light. We should also mention Philips Wouwerman (p. 104), for whom landscape was an excuse to paint horses and riders.

Isaac van Ostade, *A Frozen Canal*, p. 43
Nicolaes Berchem, *Oxen Drinking*, p. 59; *Shepherdesses*, p. 74
Aelbert Cuyp, *Landscape with Cows*, p. 22; *River Landscape*, p. 42
Philips Wouwerman, *Rest During the Falcon Hunt*, p. 104

During the second half of the century, the preference for polished surface and virtuosity rather than genuine spontaneity that is found in other areas of Dutch art extended to landscape as well. The great age of landscape, not only in Holland but elsewhere in Europe, was from 1630 to 1660. After 1660, the glamour of French and Italian painting charmed the complacent Dutch middle class, who by now loved luxury more than unadorned nature. The great Dutch landscape tradition fell into decline.

CITY SCENES

The panoramic city scene became increasingly popular in the seventeenth century, but it can be found in Dutch painting even in the fifteenth century, as a background for religious subjects. In Jan van Eyck's *Three Women at the Sepulchre*, for example, we see the city of Jerusalem silhouetted on the horizon. In his *Rollin Madonna*, a view opens through an arcade to a wide, rolling landscape divided by a river, with a city on its right. There is another such cityscape in the background of Rogier van der Weyden's *St. Luke Painting the Virgin*.

These early views of cities are fanciful. They do not depict real places but ideal ones. There is little change in the following century. Even in the work of a realist like Bruegel, city views are found only in backgrounds, and tend to be fantastic. Only in the seventeenth century does the accurate cityscape gain favor, although in most cases, cities are seen in relation to countryside or sea. It is, in fact, somewhat surprising that the theme of the city was not more popular, in this creative period when so many new subjects were being explored. The city became an important theme only later, in the work of painters, from Canaletto to Kokoschka, who treated it as a worthy subject in itself.

Jan Vermeer,
View of Delft, p. 61

The most famous seventeenth-century painting of a city, Vermeer's *View of Delft* (p. 61), was hardly noticed by his contemporaries. Nearly forgotten for almost 200 years, when it was exhibited in 1822 at a museum in The Hague, it became an immediate sensation, with the name of its creator still unknown. Although the *View of Delft* is one of Vermeer's masterpieces, it was auctioned off for the small sum of 200 guilders in 1696, twenty-one years after Vermeer's death. No reproduction can possibly convey the subtlety of its color or the degree of refinement Vermeer achieves, while at the same time giving the impression of great simplicity.

The *View of Delft* asks to be read from left to right, in the direction of the flow of water in the foreground. On the left side, we see a flat blue-white sky, a village dotted with red roofs, and then wider bands of wall, road, canal, water, and sand. This highly organized composition can also be seen as an abstraction if one chooses. Toward the right, a movement begins in the background. Two towers create a powerful contrast against a group of bright clouds. There is a burst of glittering yellow in the cottages, a line of shady trees reflected in the golden flecks on the bridge, and finally the culminating chord of the high church tower, which ends

Meindert Hobbema, *The Mill* (drawing)

this movement. Movement begins again in the red roofs and the horizontal line that runs past them, and the yellow is repeated in the foreground, which ends in the play of the light on the left. With these repetitions, movements, and countermovements, Vermeer orchestrates his composition to achieve a musically harmonious balance.

The *View of Delft* is exceptional among Vermeer's paintings. For one thing, it is his only true landscape. *A Street in Delft* should really be classified with Vermeer's interiors, because there he is concerned with the organization of geometric shapes in a cubic space. This is not true of the *View of Delft*, in which the little flecks of paint seem to have a life of their own, like the particles of light and matter they represent. Even the technique used by Vermeer in painting the *View* is different. The paint is more roughly applied; strokes are not smoothed out but set side by side, as the Impressionists later set strokes of pure color next to each other, allowing the eye to blend them. The composition is unified by the homogeneous illumination of natural daylight. The little points and dots of color suggest the movement of light across the surface of the painting, without changing the basic pattern of tones.

None of the many Dutch painters of city views came close to repeating Vermeer's triumph. Apparently, they did not even want to. For them,

Jan Vermeer,
A Street in Delft, p. 70

a work of art had a factual purpose as a kind of document or record, apart from its aesthetic merits. A city picture had to be, above all, topographically correct, which Vermeer's *View of Delft* obviously is not. It had to represent the city it portrayed with accuracy; and finally, like all paintings of the time, it had to be a clear example of the style of its creator. In the seventeenth century, there was no art for art's sake, as there is today. Art was considered to have specific social, political, and economic purposes. Today we value as works of art the paintings bought by Dutch burghers as documents, mementos, or investments. By the time of Vermeer, the Dutch social structure had solidified into rigid classes. Fifty years earlier, when Hals was painting, Holland had just won its independence from Spain, and as colonial trade and overseas possessions expanded, the young republic experienced an economic boom. The art of Hals's generation reflected the aggressive optimism and self-confidence of a people on the rise. When Vermeer was active, art had become more refined and fashionable, as the public grew more sophisticated and affluent.

Vermeer's teacher was probably Carel Fabritius, who was himself a pupil of Rembrandt. The art of Fabritius, like his view of the world, differed from that of his teacher. He was uncomfortable in Rembrandt's timeless, spaceless world of the spirit, and was more interested in surface representation than in the personality of his subject. Fabritius experimented with different effects of light. Among his known works are a number of portraits and perspective views, and he passed on an interest in perspective to his student. Fabritius, a very gifted painter, died prematurely in 1654 in the explosion of a powder magazine at Delft. Many of his paintings were destroyed in the same disaster. Two that survived, *The Goldfinch* and *Soldier Sitting on a Bench*, had been painted in the year of the artist's death. They have some characteristics that are echoed in the work of Vermeer: firm handling of the brush, a cool palette, and classical composition.

One of the most industrious painters of city views was Gerrit Adriaensz. Berckheyde. There was no major Dutch city that he did not paint with great realism and objectivity. Two of his popular scenes were *The Town Hall in Amsterdam* (p. 62), and *The Market in Haarlem* (p. 63). After the siege of Antwerp by the Spaniards in 1585, Amsterdam began to take on commercial importance. In a few decades, it developed into the most important harbor city of Europe. The proud Town Hall stood next to the New Church in the center of Amsterdam, and later became the royal palace. This staunch Town Hall was a symbol of the middle class and its puritanical strength, as well as its pride and prosperity. It was as such that Berckheyde painted it. The structure is seen facing the viewer directly, lit by the midday sun. The shadow of a tall building falls over the left half of the painting and keeps the group of figures in the foreground from completely dominating the composition. The democratic spirit of the Amsterdam burgher society is illustrated in the neighborliness of the various groups. Peddlers, journeymen, merchants on foot and on horse-

Carel Fabritius,
The Goldfinch;
Soldier Sitting
on a Bench

Gerrit Adriaensz.
Berckheyde,
The Town Hall
in Amsterdam, p. 62;
The Market
in Haarlem, p. 63

Jan Bruegel, *Harbor Tower with Sailboats* (drawing)

back, ladies and gentlemen, and a girl who has come to buy are seen
together before the Town Hall, which stands as a symbol of the repub-
lican society whose headquarters it is.

In Berckheyde's view of the Haarlem market, no single building dominates the scene. Instead, the subject is a public square whose appearance
has hardly changed from the previous century. Our gaze fastens on no
specific building, but lingers over the length and breadth of the marketplace, moving in and out among the various groups of figures to rest
finally on a road moving into the distance. We know immediately that
this is no fantasy of the painter but an accurate description of an actual
place. We focus, however, not on the beautiful Renaissance Town Hall,
but on the houses of the burghers, which symbolically dominate both city
and church.

Berckheyde's older brother, Job Adriaensz., shows a similar objectivity
in his work. Unlike his brother, he did not look for his themes in the
great public square, but in the picturesque side streets and in idyllic,
dreamy corners. In his *Canal in Delft* (p. 71), a canal boat filled with a
jolly crowd going for a Sunday boat ride occupies the mid-point of the

Job Adriaensz.
Berckheyde, *Canal
in Delft*, p. 71 57

picture. The high trees that overshadow the water cast a welcome shadow and allow the brilliant sunlight to filter through them onto the narrow side street over the bridge. An impression of happy calm is conveyed by the skillful play of light and shadow and the sun on walls and trees, while the intimacy of the scene draws the spectator into it.

Job Adriaensz. Berckheyde, *The Old Stock Exchange in Amsterdam*, p. 66

Job Berckheyde's *The Old Stock Exchange in Amsterdam* (p. 66), plunges the viewer into the center of the commercial life of the time, not only in Holland but in much of the known world. Here transactions of the Dutch East India Company took place. Here gold and precious metals were bought and sold. This was the center of trade, which brought such prosperity to Holland. In this great financial center, such native products as cheese and tulips found markets abroad, which brought prosperity even to the peasants. The sale of textiles and pottery added to the wealth of the city. Raw materials, like wool and flax, the wood and iron needed for shipbuilding, and animal fat for the soap industry had to be imported. The Amsterdam Stock Exchange, which was the Wall Street of the seventeenth century, benefited many merchants and bankers, employers and manufacturers. Here, important voyages were planned. The Exchange afforded opportunity for loss and gain, success and bankruptcy.

This is the exciting scene that Berckheyde painted. Our glance is fixed at first on the figures of two strolling brokers. The eye is led rapidly back into depth. Through the arcade, we can see the dizzying jumble of a dense crowd.

Jan Steen, *The Leyden Fish Market*, p. 67

Jan Steen, whom we know from his genre paintings of Dutch family life, brings to his densely populated city views a similar vitality and humanity. Nevertheless, buildings dominate *The Leyden Fish Market* (p. 67). Walls, cottages, and windows are painted with precise accuracy. The bridges and trees and high sky are united through a well-constructed perspective. Even without the figures, one would have an authentic image of the city; but Steen wants to paint more than picturesque scenery. He wants to convey the pulsing life of Leyden's squares and streets. He shows an astonishing diversity of life: an elegant lady, decked out with dogs and finery; fat old fishwives, drab fishermen, and wealthy merchants, crowded together with young people and tattered beggars and loafers. As contrast to the lively company, Steen shows us the dead fish. Behind the scene, around the corners of houses and the walls of canals, one can see opening again another great piazza where the viewer becomes once again involved in activity.

From the streets and public squares to the intimacy of Vermeer's *A Street in Delft* (p. 70) is a great contrast. All movement here is stilled, and the house once again becomes the place of refuge from all threats. This house needs no elegant façade; it is beautiful in itself. It is as warm and friendly as its inhabitants. People and house are in happy harmony. A woman, two sturdy children, a country maid all have their place in the order and are united through the composition. The woman relates to the open door, the children to the wall of the house, the girl to the background. The hard pavement of the street lies between the viewer and this scene of happy calm. The viewer must remain on the outside; but he can imagine what is happening within, and so participate in the lives of the people. It is a moment when time stands still.

Vermeer has achieved these subtle effects with the simplest means: only the clear, sharp light and almost shadowless brightness. Everything is realistically observed: every stone, every window shutter is recognizable. But Vermeer's is the most subjective kind of realism. Although no small detail is overlooked, the artist has transformed reality through a process of selection and abstraction, which gives it the overwhelming power of a work of art. Horizontal and vertical forms are adjusted to a complex, harmonious balance. Vermeer has so simplified forms that they approximate pure geometric volumes. For this reason, he was a favorite of the modern Cubists, who used geometry as the basis for their art. Vermeer brings us into the intimate sphere of family life. We leave public society for domestic life, seen through high walls that shield the family from the curious gaze. The family's isolation from the outside world is symbolized by the door to the inner courtyard, which opens to the enclosed garden. The color composition is based on soft harmonies of gray and orange-red, black and white, with blue, yellow, and red accents.

Nicolaes Berchem, *Oxen Drinking* (drawing)

Pieter de Hooch,
Dutch Family, p. 65

In Vermeer's *A Street in Delft,* the viewer experiences the calm of family life. In Pieter de Hooch's paintings, on the other hand, he is asked to take part in the spontaneous joy of family life. This happiness, it is clear, is achieved through hard work and a right-thinking, God-fearing life. In De Hooch's *Dutch Family* (p. 65), we see the neatly dressed, prosperous family engaged in their ordinary activities. The youngest son is interested only in his elegant clothing. The eldest is shown in the role of successful merchant and head of the house. His black clothing indicates that he belongs to the older generation. A little drama is taking place, as his wife smiles coquettishly in her richly embroidered red-and-gold gown. In this painting, as in many others, De Hooch gives the illusion of deep space by setting spaces within spaces; the open door offers a view into the garden, inviting us into its expanse. Pieter de Hooch's paintings are an example of one of the loveliest specializations cultivated by the Dutch painters in the seventeenth century: genre painting, which recreates scenes of ordinary contemporary life.

In his book on Dutch painting, Jean Leymarie insists that the theme is neither the individual nor even history with its myths and heroes, but daily life. This was a relatively new theme in European art. In the late Middle Ages, of course, there were genre elements, especially in Nativity scenes, which often showed Joseph engaged in some domestic activity or the midwife getting ready the bathwater. The great age of genre painting, however, began with Hieronymus Bosch and Pieter Bruegel, although in their paintings, scenes of daily life were meant to carry a message or teach a moral. Lucas van Leyden, a sixteenth-century Dutch painter, filled his religious pictures with genre themes. He and others, like Cornelisz Anthonisz. and Pieter Aertsen, who specialized in kitchen and market scenes, helped to bring about the triumph of genre painting.

In Italy, the painting of daily life first became popular in the seventeenth century. It became important in France only in the eighteenth century, chiefly as the lovers' picnic or some such theme removed from everyday life. Classicism had other tasks to perform. In German romantic painting and in the Biedermeier period of the early nineteenth century, true genre painting was rediscovered. In the work of the early Impressionists, above all in Manet, genre elements again made their appearance. These genre elements, however, became submerged when Impressionism blossomed in the work of Monet, Renoir, and Sisley. In the antibourgeois art of the twentieth century, genre painting naturally has no place. Today, it is confined to caricature or social satire.

The seventeenth century remains the great period of genre painting, that epoch in which the middle class triumphed. There were two main types of Dutch genre painting at mid-century: a folkish, lower-middle-class version, and an intimate, aristocratic variety. The latter bloomed in Leyden, and above all in Delft, the city where the fine blue faïence pattern was made. Delft was a center of cultured taste and refined life style. It was the birthplace of Vermeer, but one should remember that two other great painters, Carel Fabritius and Pieter de Hooch worked

Jan Vermeer, *View of Delft*

On the following pages:

Gerrit Adriaensz. Berckheyde, *The Town Hall in Amsterdam*
Gerrit Adriaensz. Berckheyde, *The Market in Haarlem*

Pieter de Hooch, *Dutch Family*

Pieter de Hooch, *The Mother* (detail)
Right: Gabriel Metsu, *The Letter Writer*

On the preceding pages:

Job Adriaensz. Berckheyde, *The Old Stock Exchange in Amsterdam*
Jan Steen, *The Leyden Fish Market*

Jan Vermeer, *A Street in Delft*

Right: Job Adriaensz. Berckheyde, *Canal in Delft*

there, too. De Hooch, the son of a Rotterdam mason, was born in 1629. A pupil of Nicolaes Berchem in Haarlem, De Hooch must have lacked interest in landscape, because we know no landscape by him. At twenty, he ended his apprenticeship and enlisted in the service of a Leyden draper as a "master painter" and servant. In 1653, he arrived in Delft, where he joined the painters' guild. A year later, he married the daughter of a Delft faïence painter. This was his happiest and most fruitful year. His friendship with Vermeer stimulated him, and his happy family life gave him a secure atmospere in which to work. His masterpieces, about forty in number, were produced during these years between his marriage and the move to Amsterdam in 1666. What befell De Hooch at this time we do not know, but his artistic development was doomed from this moment on. Until his death, apparently in 1684, he did not create another important work.

De Hooch's *Outdoor Company* (p. 86), is another of his typical inner courtyard scenes, a kind of group portrait in a family situation. Only four figures are in the scene: a man, two women, and then, at a distance, a serving girl. The picture tells no story. There are few clues to help the viewer reconstruct what is happening. In any event, all this is unimportant to the meaning of the picture, which is meant to appeal to the eye and the sense of touch. Different textures and materials of various thicknesses and qualities are emphasized. There is wood, stone, metal, and glass. In his careful rendering of these materials, De Hooch transforms the everyday into something unusual. The paleness of the evening light helps to effect this transformation by gilding the scene with a golden patina, but this alone does not explain its magic, which lies much deeper. It is the feeling of happiness and contentment conveyed by this painting that arouses in the viewer a similar feeling of well-being and makes him appreciate the things of this world, the simple reality of the everyday. In Vermeer's *A Street in Delft*, we participate in the same kind of happiness.

De Hooch is equally well known for his paintings of interiors. The intimacy of such scenes takes place in the interior space of family rooms. The great part of De Hooch's work is involved with the depiction of such classical interior spaces. Since Jan van Eyck's *Arnolfini Wedding Portrait*, the middle-class interior had been a popular subject. Here, 200 years before De Hooch, Van Eyck represented the typical Dutch interior,

Pieter de Hooch, *Outdoor Company*, p. 86

Gerard Terborch, *The Apple Peeler*

Nicolaes Berchem, *Shepherdesses* (sketch)

Pieter de Hooch, *The Mother*, p. 68

with its alcoves, open windows through which light streams, mirror, and intimate details, like the pair of shoes left behind. The Master of Flémalle, as well, included details of contemporary interiors in religious paintings. In the fifteenth century, religious figures were seen in contemporary settings. (What painter of our time would show a Nativity in modern dress?)

The influence of Italian painters on the Dutch changed the style of domestic interiors. The middle-class living room was seen in terms of the Italian Renaissance. Again, it was only Bruegel who continued to paint native interiors. So we see that De Hooch's interiors came out of a long tradition. But De Hooch did not use the interior as a decorative milieu in which to set a scene; he represented it for its own sake as the greatest expression of the new middle-class life styles. This life style prized not only joy in order and solid prosperity, but also the inner freedom and well-being that has analogies in the lucid space of the De Hooch interiors. Here everything is sober and orderly; yet the place does not seem to be cold. Everything is cozy and friendly. In the painting *The Mother* (p. 68), the open alcove, through which we see a rumpled bed, introduces a hint of disorder into this tidy world. Here, too, we find De Hooch's characteristic ordering of space—a succession of parallel planes seen through open doors, a recurrent motive in his work. In this picture, the living room, the kitchen, and the courtyard are bound together through the light that filters into them. In order to give an even greater impression of deep space, De Hooch has traced an imaginary line from the right corner of the painting, passing through the two hands of the woman, the head of the little girl, and over the half-shut door, directing our gaze into the distance. A second line pulls the eye from the left corner of the painting, over the feet of the tables, toward the door. It meets a third line that begins somewhere in the middle of the painting and passes over the feet of the woman, the dog, the child, and through the courtyard door. This movement into depth is balanced by the many strong horizontal elements, such as the lines of the flagstones in the living room. Such a geometrical construction of space allows De Hooch to achieve an exhilarating clarity and harmonious tranquillity, without disturbing the general feeling of warmth. The local colors—above all, De Hooch's beloved red and golden brown—are made more brilliant by the rays of light that cross the picture, casting shadows and throwing reflections.

In *The Linen Closet* (p. 82), De Hooch takes us into a tidy, middle-class household. He shows us the housewife with her costly possessions. In the heavy oak-and-ebony closet (an actual piece of furniture of a middle-class household of the period), Flemish linens and elegant silks from the East Indies were stored. A typical burgher of that time possessed 60 bed covers, 30 tablecloths, and more than 300 napkins.

Pieter de Hooch,
The Linen Closet,
p. 82

There are other signs of prosperity, presented with a certain pride. On the walls, pictures hang; door and window moldings are decorated with pilasters. The basin above the closet is decorated with many colors. There is even a piece of ancient sculpture. Through the open door of the house there is a view of the canal, as if to demonstrate that this is an elegant neighborhood. Even the dresses of the two women suggest prosperity; and the child in the background wears a rich dress in patrician style. The scene is set in an antechamber; we can see other rooms leading from it, and an elegant staircase lighted from above.

The figure of the woman occupies the middle of the picture. She inhabits her intimate environment and wears her expensive clothes, not as a sign of social standing, but as an expression of her distinguished life style.

De Hooch had a narrow range of themes, but a great sense of space and composition. The human figure was not important for him; what was important was the inhabited room or garden with its clear, ordered spaces, made all the more convincing by his mastery of perspective. He began his compositions with the architectural framework, then fit his figures into it. His primary interest was space and the abstract patterns created by blocks of colors. In treatment of interior space he differs from Vermeer. De Hooch's compositions are based on a continuous series of cubic spaces, rather than on a single space divided by figures and furniture. His figures are not as monumental and silent as those of Vermeer. His art seems more intimate, warmer, and perhaps more human than that of his contemporary in Delft.

In De Hooch's paintings, sunlight falls on bricks and tiles, enriching colors with a warm glow. He delighted in the possessions and the order that typified the Dutch spirit of the time. The clean, sunny rooms, suffused with air and light from open doors and windows, are the setting for a happy, well-regulated life. It has been said that De Hooch was like a cat who prefers the house to its inhabitants.

In his late work he, too, succumbed to the taste for luxury and pretention. The paintings became crowded and the coloring flat and drab by comparison with the sparkle of his early works. Trying to keep up with the fashionable painters of the *tableau de mode* (genre pictures of upper-middle-class manners), De Hooch also introduced amorous motifs in his late works.

No Dutch painter of interiors was as successful at realizing interior space as Pieter de Hooch. By contrast, in the work of a painter of interiors like Gabriel Metsu, interior space has no formal or intellectual meaning of its own; man always remains the center. Humanity is the focus of Metsu's art.

Born in Leyden in 1629, Metsu may have studied with Gerard Dou, a painter of fashionable genre pictures and a pupil of Rembrandt. Dou was also a native of Leyden, where he was born in 1613. He worked carefully, and his meticulous details and polished surfaces were very popular. Dou studied with Rembrandt for three years. His family probably wanted him to learn portrait painting, which was Rembrandt's lucrative speciality. Rembrandt's pupils painted their teacher's father and mother and posed for one another. Like their master, they painted hermits and saints reading in a strong light. The influence of Honthorst of Utrecht can also be discerned in Dou's student works. The hermit motif, a typical picturesque subject, reappears in his late paintings.

When Rembrandt left Leyden for Amsterdam in 1631, Dou began to paint realistic genre scenes. By this time, he was so famous that the Swedish ambassador to Amsterdam, a great art patron of the period, paid him for an option on everything he painted. In 1640, Dou developed a theme that greatly increased his popularity. He began to paint so-called niche pieces, each representing a view through a window into a room. In these works, he often used a device learned in Rembrandt's studio: he lighted the inner room or the sill with a candle, creating a nighttime counterpart to the daytime niche piece. In his last years, Dou recorded the entire repertory of items from middle-class homes in his niche pictures. He smoothed over his brushstroke to present a glossy, uniform surface. By contrast, Rembrandt was slashing his paint into the canvas with a palette knife, a thumb, or a paintbrush. His golden shadows ate away at his forms, eliminating unnecessary detail.

In 1660, the city of Leyden bought three of Dou's paintings as gifts for Charles II. Later, the king invited the artist to work for him in England, but Dou refused, being far too comfortable where he was. When he died at 62, he left a fortune.

Metsu was but one of Dou's successful pupils. At fifteen, he was a member of the Leyden branch of the Guild of St. Luke, but he soon moved to Amsterdam, attracted to the great metropolis like many artists from provincial schools. He married and later died there, at the age of 36. Metsu's early work reflects Dou's influence. His surfaces have a high finish, and objects are shown precisely as they appear. He borrowed Dou's formula of representing figures behind a window sill. Most of Metsu's paintings are domestic scenes.

When Metsu settled in Amsterdam, he became a painter of the high bourgeoisie. Rembrandt was living in Amsterdam at the time, and his style influenced Metsu, who imitated the master's chiaroscuro technique and use of color.

One of his best-known works, *The Letter Writer* (p. 69), shows the influence of Vermeer. Through a wide open window comes a bright flood of light that illuminates the space and the figure of a seated young man. At first glance, the youth appears totally self-absorbed and involved with his own activities, like the figures in Vermeer's interiors. A closer look reveals that he is oddly posed, there appears to be little relationship between his body and the stool he is sitting on. No one who was really writing a letter would sit that way in front of a desk. The boy's stiff pose looks unnatural. It is the pose of a painter who arranges everything for the greatest decorative effect. As for the inner life, Metsu seems to have no insight. He is much more interested in the artistic possibilities of objects and their relationship to the human figure than in human psychology. He delights in rich carpets, the play of light and shadow on sparkling pewter, the glass window with its reflections, and, in the dark corner, the globe that receives reflected light. The young man is dressed in a garment whose elegance lies in its simplicity. A dark coat, dark stockings, dark shoes are set off by the bright white shirt, with its dandy-like puffs and frills. Such effective contrasts are masterfully arranged throughout the painting: the dark carpet against the deep shadows; the brown of the globe against the light brown of the window; the shining glasses against the dark background; and the pale face against the dusky wall. This face has a pale, girlish beauty, and looks almost bleached in comparison with the rich colors around it.

The comparative weakness of Metsu's skill with interiors is seen in his painting of *The Geelvink Family* (p. 83). Here is another merchant's family, like those in De Hooch's family portraits. But De Hooch shows us personalities and unique inner life, while Metsu depicts no more than a group of unresponsive figures, a wealthy merchant's family with their children's nurse. The house, although undistinguished as architecture, is crowded with silks, tapestries, and expensive paintings. The heavy furniture and the whole family, in their rich clothing, complete the picture. Middle-class pride has become bourgeois complacency; the enjoyment of prosperity has become ostentation; proportion and moderation have

Gabriel Metsu,
The Letter Writer,
p. 69

Gabriel Metsu,
The Geelvink Family,
p. 83

77

Gerard Terborch, *Study*
(drawing)

become extravagance. A new generation has matured, for whom the challenges of war and independence are now mere history. This generation has merely inherited its fathers' possessions, enjoying freedom without having had to earn it. Here is the first indication of decadence in a splendid period.

As in *The Letter Writer,* Metsu demonstrates in this family picture his skill at painting materials. The glowing silk, the jewelry, and the feathers are all imbued with a life of their own; the care with which they are painted suggests that the real interest of the artist was in these showy possessions, rather than in individual human beings, who are presented as stereotypes, without warmth or life.

Although the cool restraint that we noticed in De Hooch is missing in Metsu, we find it again in the work of Gerard Terborch, who was fascinated, like Metsu, with the precious and beautiful things. Terborch's pictures are usually group genre scenes, although he did some still lifes as well, in which the composition is strong enough to offset the richness of ornamental detail. Despite Terborch's fanatical realism, his pictures never degenerate into mere accumulations of detail. Terborch's *The Apple Peeler* (p. 72) represents a static situation. All movement is stilled; the eye must accept the inconvenience of making out forms in this glowing dusk. How does Terborch express his meaning? Through the architectonic construction of the composition: a strong system of horizontals and verticals creates a sense of tranquillity. Typically, Terborch uses the figure of a woman as the focus of his paintings. A single moment is frozen here—as in a photograph—as the action of the apple peeler, whose left hand is suspended in tension, is brought to a halt. Above all, we are impressed with the harmony of objects and figures. No trivial detail disturbs the scene. In this context, material objects take on greater value. The clothing no longer serves merely to decorate the figure; it has its own meaning in Terborch's work. The delicate porcelain, coarse woollens, the light tulle, fur, embroidery, feathers, and flesh are all represented by the artist with the highest delicacy and understanding. Yet, despite this, he allows the people to express their own individuality.

Gerard Terborch was born in 1617 in Zwolle. The son of a tax collector, he traveled to England, Spain, France, Germany, and Italy. With his family connections and education, he was able to gain entrance into the highest society. In this cultivated atmosphere, he developed a love for all that was beautiful and precious, without ever losing his innate spontaneity. His aristocratic spirit never lost itself in ostentation, but continued to maintain the most distinguished restraint and the most refined technique.

Active mainly in Haarlem, Terborch painted the soldiers and cavaliers so popular as themes in the 1630's. His pictures are polite, elegant, and dignified. Even his peddlers and workmen look like aristocrats doing manual labor by mistake. Terborch is always worldly and tasteful. His women are charming, lazy, and a bit bored, like Dutch society itself in the second half of the century. They engage in such upper-class occupations as letter-writing, music-making, and socializing. Typically, Terborch illuminates his balance with a cool gray light that is enlivened by the shimmer of silks and satins. Terborch's space is shallower than that of De Hooch, and the people tend to be more important than their setting, while quite the opposite is true of De Hooch's paintings. This is not surprising, because, unlike De Hooch, Terborch was an important painter of portraits, as well.

Most of the important Dutch genre painters depicted the untroubled beauty and security of middle-class family life; only Rembrandt was a master of psychological drama. While his contemporaries were content to portray man's everyday activities, Rembrandt studied man's inner life. It is interesting to see that even Rembrandt's pupils and followers, such as Nicolaes Maes, Jan Lievens, or Govaert Flinck, were unable to sustain

Gerard Terborch, *The Apple Peeler*, p. 72

79

his concentration on the spiritual in their paintings and in such drawings as Maes's *Woman Praying* (p. 106) or his *Woman Spinning* (p. 154). Like most of their contemporaries, Rembrandt's pupils and followers specialized in gentle, quiet, decorative scenes, or charming, picturesque genre paintings, such as Maes's *The Naughty Drummer* (p. 81).

Nicolas Maes was born in Amsterdam in 1632. He worked in Rembrandt's studio from 1650 to 1665, when he went to Antwerp. After his return to Amsterdam, he did portraits in the aristocratic style popular in Flanders. His style had changed so radically that later scholars conjured up a "Maes of Brussels" to explain the transformation.

Throughout the artist's early years, however, Rembrandt's influence was apparent. Maes, too, was a master technician, and his forms, like those of Rembrandt, seemed to emerge from dark space. His compositions were illuminated by daylight or firelight, which played in and out of the shadows like the light in the compositions of his mentor. His palette was limited. Maes used black and white to plot his design and often splashed red against grayish blues and purples.

A favorite subject of Maes's was the eavesdropper: a woman spying on lovers, a servant on his employers. *Lovers with a Woman Listening* is the title of one such painting. It is not surprising that his work pleased the public more than Rembrandt's stormy dramas.

Nicolaes Maes, *Woman Praying*, p. 106; *Woman Spinning*, p. 154; *The Naughty Drummer*, p. 81

Nicolaes Maes, *Lovers with a Woman Listening*

Nicolaes Maes, *The Naughty Drummer* 81

Pieter de Hooch, *The Linen Closet*

Gabriel Metsu, *The Geelvink Family*

Hendrick Terbrugghen, *The Flute Player*

Right: Johannes Cornelisz. Verspronck, *Girl in a Blue Dress* (detail)

Pieter de Hooch, *Outdoor Company*

Gerard Terborch, *The Concert*

Frans Hals, *Malle Babbe*

A genre painting can be understood as an anonymous group portrait. We do not know who the persons in a genre scene may be. They represent types rather than individuals: a mother, a child, a soldier, a lady. The artist introduces them in order to make general statements about the human condition. He paints a peasant, a cavalier, or a tavern maid in terms of costume and behavior, as a general type with specific recognizable characteristics. Movement is important to genre. The heroic can impress us in its static monumentality, but the intimate, which is the sphere of genre, can claim our attention only through movement. According to Friedländer: "The painter who feels the universal human constant naturally inclines to the lower classes, whose doings and behavior are not regulated by education and ceremonial." Peasants and children are more or less the same through the ages. Because of this, Bruegel's, Brouwer's, and Van Ostade's peasant scenes seem truer to us today than the fashionable genre paintings of the second half of the century by painters like Terborch and Metsu, with their emphasis on costumes and fancy manners.

In order not to dominate the small rooms of the seventeenth-century Dutch houses where they hung, genre paintings had to be small in scale. Usually, themes were simple, because those who purchased such works wanted to take in the drama in a single glance. Like many art buyers today, the typical Dutch collector was more interested in the artist's subject than in how well he painted.

One great influence on the development of low-life genre painting, as distinguished from domestic genre, was the Italian painter Michelangelo Merisi, known as Caravaggio. A realist whose subjects were humble people in humble surroundings, Caravaggio is supposed to have said "I paint nature." His primary interests, however, were the human figure and light. He discovered an irrational system of lighting that came to be known as "cellar light" because of its dimness. Caravaggio's paintings, however, unlike their Dutch counterparts, are really religious paintings disguised as low-life genre. His *Calling of St. Matthew*, which takes place in a tavern, is an example of one such work.

Adriaen van Ostade, *The Bowling Alley* (drawing)

The fact that Dutch painters respected the lowly themes of peasant life may be taken as a sign of their optimism. For them, everything in creation, no matter how humble, was worth painting. Genre painting implies that man is enjoying life and that he values himself and his possessions sufficiently to wish to preserve them in art. But sometimes, the Dutch artists who painted low-life genre scenes went beyond simple enjoyment to display a mischievous delight in shocking the middle-class buyers of their art, in the same way that Toulouse-Lautrec was to shock the middle class with his brothels and dance halls two centuries later. This tendency to delight in the naughty is most apparent in the paintings of Adriaen Brouwer, whose principal subjects were free-living peasants, enjoying a style of life that would have scandalized the tidy and frugal middle-class. Brouwer was born in Flanders, but we count him among the Dutch masters because he settled in Holland at an early age. At sixteen, in Antwerp, he was a student of Pieter Bruegel, the younger; but by the time he was twenty, he had gone to Amsterdam. A year later, he was in Haarlem, where he became a pupil of Frans Hals. Brouwer was as direct and frank as Hals, but even wilder in his choice of subjects. His people grimace and chortle without inhibition. In his later work, he avoided caricature in order to focus on moods. His colors became softer and more harmonious, and he took greater advantage of chiaroscuro to soften contours. The poverty of the surroundings he depicts is made more vivid by the richness of his colors and of his technique.

Brouwer could never be taken for an intellectual painter, but his paintings are full of life. He was a heavy drinker who loved the grotesque appearance of his drinking companions and caricatured these debauched or detestable creatures with sure, beautiful draftsmanship. The color in Brouwer's early work was based on harmonies of local color. Bright yellow and red were often combined with neutral grays and browns, as well as green and pale red. As he became more of a "tonal" painter, who graduated and modulated his color instead of applying it flatly, Brouwer used a deep green in the foreground, with graded reds, blues, and violets, as well as drab neutral colors. In Brouwer's late work, on the other hand, a grayish black tonality prevails, and color, when it occurs, is merely used as an accent.

Brouwer, one of the greatest of the Dutch painters, whose free, brushy technique distinguished his style, died bankrupt in 1638. Among the few who valued his work were Rubens and Rembrandt, who understood the difference between a worthless subject and a valuable painting. Others, less sensitive to purely aesthetic values, however, saw in Brouwer only his low subject matter. Today, a pop artist such as Claes Oldenburg is once again attempting, like Brouwer, to produce great art from humble subjects. Rubens owned seventeen of Brouwer's paintings, and Rembrandt owned eight, in addition to a sketchbook of his drawings. Like Hals, Brouwer could capture the essence of a subject in a quick sketch. His mind, hand, and eye worked together to record lively scenes in taverns and brothels, because his subjects were not likely to pose for him. Brouwer's subjects were no proud, prosperous merchants, but the scum of the underworld. These were the poorest peasants and artisans, with an occasional soldier or young ruffian. Women—or at least the young and the beautiful—were virtually excluded from his work. The women he painted were aging and hideous, as drunken and drugged with tobacco and wine as the ragged men who accompanied them. The rooms were ugly and shabby, the furnishing primitive and drab, and the people ordinary, rumpled, and simple. Cracks in the walls, windows falling apart, a dirty tablecloth, stockings falling down, hats awry—and despite, or perhaps because of all this, what fascinating pictures!

Card-Playing Peasants in the Tavern is appealing because of its liveliness, its spontaneity, its fresh naturalism, and, above all, because of the genius of its composition, which balances areas of light and dark and locks forms securely into place. A light, yellowish brown bathes all the figures with color. In front of this almost monochrome background, colors and values stand out in sharp relief. The three chords of contrasting color— red, blue, and green—are built up in a rich play of light. Against the broken white of the blouse, these colors seem even brighter and clearer. All the tones are illuminated by the play of light on the cards and shirts, which also creates deep shadows.

Adriaen Brouwer,
*Card-Playing Peasants
in the Tavern*, p. 100

Adriaen van Ostade,
Peasant Gathering
(drawing)

Adriaen Brouwer,
The Performance,
p. 98

Brouwer gets the maximum dramatic meaning from the light in a picture like *The Performance* (p. 98). A narrow stage becomes the background for the joyful fiddler and the sad company of old men in the background. Although quite tipsy, they are still able to participate in the cheerful music. The singing power of the light that Brouwer brought into his mischievous satire would again be realized by Rembrandt, a generation later. The influence of Adriaen Brouwer on contemporary art was immediate. He gave painters a new series of scenes, which had been virtually forgotten since Bruegel. With the power of genius, he had uncovered a whole new world, which had formely lain in the shadows of middle-class prosperity. Now the inhabitants of this underworld were glorified in art: the drinker, the debtor, the gambler, and the drifter. The scintillating life of the tavern and the streets was celebrated by Brouwer as a challenge to the world of bourgeois prosperity. The middle class, however, enjoyed the spectacle of tramps and drunks. They saw the rude manners and wild life of the lower classes as a curiosity. Pleasure in their own polished manners and comfortable surroundings was enhanced by contrast.

Adriaen van Ostade, although only five years younger than Brouwer, was very much influenced by him in his early works. He, too, lived in Haarlem and worked with Frans Hals. Until 1640, he painted subjects typical of Brouwer in Brouwer's style: shabby groups of peasants in dark hats and rough costumes, engaged in drinking and dancing. After Brouwer's death, Van Ostade quickly changed his style. His scenes became more agreeable, his technique more polished, and his peasant types more amusing than vulgar. Shortly after the death of his first wife in 1638, Van Ostade had married a woman of better status than his own, which may account for a further change, from vulgar subjects to more elegant ones. With the new subject matter, his colors lost their magic power to reflect light. His palette grew duller and his themes more trivial, but Van Ostade resisted the temptation to lose himself in charming details by handling paint with a fresh vitality and exercising rich creative fantasy. Van Ostade's *The Violin Player* (p. 97) shows the great difference between him and Brouwer. What Brouwer achieved through the dramatic, Van Ostade represents with quiet contemplation. Here the drunken group is shown against the symbols of ruin: the cracked wall and the broken window. The drinker, the jovial wit, the poor but honest violin player, the workmen, and finally the children, quite at home in their debauched surroundings, are presented in a true genre picture, without satiric implications. It imparts the same warm and binding feeling that we get from the middle-class group portrait of the time. The composition is carefully developed: sharp diagonals give a sense of liveliness and of depth. The principal diagonal runs from the lower left-hand corner over the boy in the foreground, and over the figure of the drinker to the pipe-smoking tavern owner; this imaginary line pulls the eye into the dark background. Parallel to this line run two short diagonals, one uniting the dog, the two children, and the flask, and the other running through the violin. A countermovement is set up by the line passing through the violin and the low bench at the lower right. This line meets the principal diagonal in the mug of the drinker, the symbolical as well as the compositional center of the picture. In this small space, there are no fewer than eleven persons, in addition to countless details of architecture and objects. Yet despite this, the scene never looks overcrowded, which shows Van Ostade's great power to order his compositions. His rich palette of colors, above all, the light cool green tones and the warm browns, is used here toward constructive ends. Van Ostade was no social satirist, but a detached realist, a great storyteller who created his own world. His realism and highly ordered compositions recall the paintings of Jan Steen. For his representation, too, we always have a definite sense of purpose.

Van Ostade's scenes of tavern and peasant life are not far from pure painted literature. They are examples of an imagined reality. His paintings cannot be taken in at first glance. One has to study them for a while in order to see their entirety, which is never merely ugly or merely beautiful. For Jan Steen's work, too, there are always unexpected elements. Expensively dressed people sit in some shabby room, without seeming to notice

Adriaen van Ostade,
The Violin Player,
p. 97

93

their vulgar surroundings. In fact, they are having a good time. Steen showed the beautiful only by contrast. A laughing face, a well-constructed, powerful body are found on a drunk. The silhouette of an elegant woman is seen in decadent company. Goodness is seen in such a context as someone drowning helplessly in a sea of squalor. But Steen was no moralist. He painted the world as he saw it, without judging what he saw. He loved storytelling, and he provided many anecdotal details in the genre paintings he made in Leyden, The Hague, Haarlem, and Delft. Because his style shows little development, experts have trouble dating his works. Humor and wit are what make Steen remarkable and appealing. Like some modern artists, he achieved the highest dramatic effect through contrast. Steen's paintings are full of double meanings, of ambiguities. People seem to be playing roles, as in the theater. Behind the magic of the scintillating beauty, there is a hint of yawning emptiness. Steen shows both good and evil in human nature. He contrasts naïve spontaneity with sophisticated joy and sorrow. The greatness of his best art, however, lies in its refreshing humor and in the artist's provocation to happy, vital laughter. Laughter and amorous gaiety play the important role we might expect in the work of a brewer's son. A brewer himself, and during his last years an innkeeper, who operated a tavern in Leyden, Steen included many piquant and frivolous anecdotes in his work.

Isaac van Ostade,
Peasants and Wagon
(drawing)

Paulus Potter, *Animals* (drawing)

Steen was born in Leyden in 1626. He grew up there while Rembrandt was achieving fame in his native town and in Amsterdam. Rembrandt had no direct influence on Steen's artistic development, however. The older artist's subjective approach had little appeal for the less poetic Steen, who loved the direct and the ordinary. By 1649, Steen had moved to The Hague, where he married the daughter of Jan van Goyen, the famous landscape painter. He was respected as a citizen and esteemed as a painter, but was less successful as a brewer. In 1657, he had to liquidate his business. In 1661, he went to Haarlem, where he stayed only a few years, and then returned, this time permanently, to his native Leyden, where he opened an inn. In 1673, he married for the second time, four years after the death of his first wife. By the time of his death in 1679, his works had become a mere echo of what they had once been. With his painting *The Crazy Company* (p. 101), Steen took up again a theme that Bosch had investigated 150 years earlier and that Pieter Bruegel had painted as "the world upside down." But the religious humanistic meanings of these two are no longer suggested. Steen's figures are divorced from the real world around him. His crazy company is animated by raucous liveliness.

Jan Steen,
The Crazy Company,
p. 101

They show the whole range of the absurd and the unexpected. Here is the little domestic world turned topsy-turvy. Here, the housewife, symbol of highest order, is shown fast asleep, undoubtedly full of sweet wine. The signs of discipline—swords, rods, and sticks—hang askew. The household is in a state of anarchy. A monkey plays with the clock on the wall, disturbing even the marking of time. The children play wildly. A dog eats on the table, undisturbed. A young man throws "roses before swine." Wine flows from the cask. Objects lie helter-skelter. In the midst of this disorder sits a disorderly company. A musician plays to the sleeping housewife, who can't hear him anyhow. A "professor" reads to another woman, but she ignores him, to indicate how little wisdom is valued here. Instead, she flirts with the young man, who in turn teases the girl with the wine glass. None of these people relates to any other. Each is involved with himself. They have their own dreams and ambitions. They do not communicate with one another. Outer chaos signifies inner chaos. Hope blooms only in the figure of the young girl. She alone has no part in the disorder. Smiling and happy, she seems to be a symbol of reason in this strange setting. Her smile suggests the artist's attitude. He does not admonish, but indicates with humor he ludicrousness of the scene.

Jan Steen, *The Baker Oostwaard*, p. 102

In contrast, Steen's painting of *The Baker Oostwaard* (p. 102) is a tribute to the upright working life. Without pathos, but with a certain pride, this simple workman shows us how he enjoys the happiness of his existence. He is shown with his pretty, well-dressed wife, a small urchin, and a quantity of loaves. The baker's drab working clothes contrast with his wife's elegant costume and earrings. The contrast is one of externals. The family is clearly bound together in harmonious unity.

Jan Steen, *Tavern Garden*, p. 99

Steen's *Tavern Garden* (p. 99) is also overflowing with life, but set within a specific space. This is not a peasant tavern but a good middle-class tavern. In the foreground, we see a happy family picnic. The husband feeds his dog with part of the fish he is eating; the wife gives her child something to drink. Behind them, the fish peddler laughs happily. Again, we have a scene without hidden meaning or irony. Steen describes every detail with uncompromising realism. The still life of things to eat on the table, the dog, the curved flask in the foreground, are all observed with loving attention. The man in the foreground may, in fact, be Steen himself; and the woman opposite, his wife, Margaret. At any rate, the man resembles a self-portrait by Steen. This man's sympathetic expression, his good-natured laugh, his open gaze and worldy manner would seem to befit the creator of so many lively paintings of lower-class Dutch life.

Adriaen van Ostade, *The Violin Player*   97

Adriaen Brouwer, *The Performance*

Jan Steen, *Tavern Garden*

Adriaen Brouwer, *Card-Playing Peasants in the Tavern*

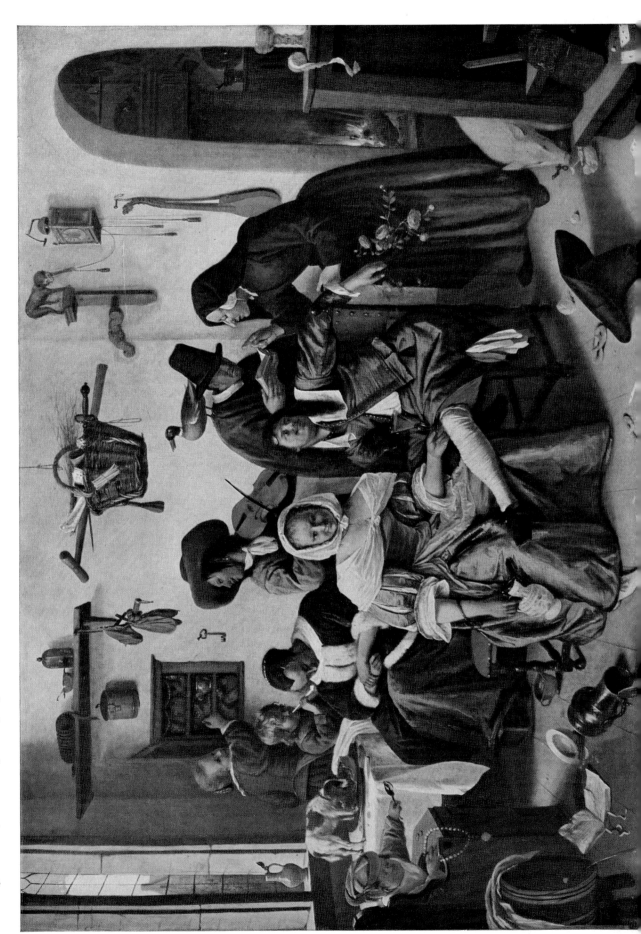

Jan Steen, *The Crazy Company*

Jacob Gerritsz. Cuyp, *Two Children with a Lamb*

Left: Jan Steen, *The Baker Oostwaard*

In genre paintings, man is always related to the environment. We learn to recognize him in his native landscape—in the streets and public squares of his city, in the circle of his family, as the proud head of the household. We find him in his private world and in public, in peasant cottages, in grand middle-class homes, and in dark taverns. We can form a picture of the life and customs of a people from all these sources; but to know them as individuals we must look at their portraits. In every period of artistry, as much in painting as in sculpture, human portraits have a special meaning. The way that he sees himself tells us something about man's desires. Portraits represent intimate documents of the human soul that, in the course of time, speak to us of the spiritual life of a specific period. The most important artists of a period usually give a principal place in their work to the portrait. Only they had the talent to master this difficult theme. Van Eyck, Raphael, Leonardo da Vinci, Titian, Dürer, Rubens, and Velasquez were all great portrait painters. In the seventeenth century, two of the three greatest painters in Holland, Frans Hals and Rembrandt, were portraitists. Holland, in this period, was the most fruitful place for the development of portraiture. The Reformation and humanism had elevated the individual to a high role in spiritual and religious affairs. National independence and self-assurance gave him an even greater freedom. His personal destiny was now dependent on his own initiative and happiness. He had only to develop his personality to achieve success. The portrait was an ideal means of glorifying this individuality. It was also a profitable specialty, because the prosperous merchants and bankers, who wanted portraits as a symbol of their prestige, were able to pay high prices for the paintings they commissioned. Because there were more

Philips Wouwerman, *Rest During the Falcon Hunt*

Nicolaes Maes,
Woman Praying
(drawing)

possibilities for portrait commissions in wealthy commercial centers like Amsterdam, Rembrandt moved there from his birthplace, Leyden; there, for a decade, he was one of the most successful painters of portraits. With the money he earned, he was able to buy a house and to assemble an important art collection.

We would have an imcomplete idea of the period if we confined our study to portraits of distinguished people. Many portraits of unknown men show us an even greater individuality, free of all convention. Often, these anonymous portraits are lusty, uncultivated, and natural. Brouwer, for example, painted half-length portraits of ugly peasants. Gerard Dou painted sad old crones, and Frans Hals painted boisterous drinkers like his famous *Malle Babbe* (p. 88), who looks like the most gossipy and quarrelsome drunk of her time. Hals paints her as a dangerous but imposing old witch, with a big mug of beer in front of her. On her shoulder, an owl perches. Set against a sad, gray-brown background, she is shocking in her ugliness. Yet she is full of the vitality of the common people. She seems to relish her freedom, the freedom she shares with Dutch people of every class. With *Malle Babbe*, Hals showed his independence of the

Frans Hals,
Malle Babbe, p. 88

106

taste of his time. In this picture, his fantasy prompted him to single out a scurrilous old lady and to paint her with as much care as the most important model.

One of the most attractive themes of portraiture of this time was the child. The great family feeling of the Dutch went so far as to encompass the world of the child. In the seventeenth century, the theme of the child, which the later Middle Ages treated in the Christ-child, had a kind of middle-class renaissance. In every Dutch genre painting, we find such a child. There are children in the paintings of Pieter de Hooch, Jan Steen, and Nicolaes Maes. In Vermeer's painting, *A Street in Delft* (p. 70), there are two children, and his *Girl with the Pearl* (p. 145) is one of the most beautiful representations of youthful charm. Johannes Cornelisz. Verspronck, a student of Frans Hals and a successful portrait painter in Holland, paints a type of child (p. 85) we don't see again, a wide-awake, self-conscious person, highly introspective, and confident of status. This child knows that she comes from a good family, that she is dressed in expensive clothes, and that her pearls are real. She also knows what she wants. The assured pose of her small, energetic hands suggests as much. Despite this, she remains a child. Her wide eyes and transparent complexion give her the naïve charm that is the enchantment of childhood.

The children of Jacob Gerritsz. Cuyp's painting, *Two Children with a Lamb* (p. 103) are, in contrast, quite different. Beneath the sweet impression of childish guilelessness, there is a whole layer of deeply meaningful allegory. The lamb in the middle of the picture is the symbol of innocence. Out of the darkness comes the head of a goat, a symbol of evil. On the ground lie pearls and mussels, allegories for vanity and mutability. The children, dressed as shepherds, anticipate the pastoral scenes that will become so important in the succeeding century. Despite these intellectual overtones, they remain two children, regarding us from a golden warmth that spreads itself over the whole scene.

Jan Vermeer, *A Street in Delft*, p. 70;
Girl with the Pearl, p. 145
Johannes Cornelisz. Verspronck, *Girl in a Blue Dress*, p. 85

Jacob Gerritsz. Cuyp, *Two Children with a Lamb*, p. 103

107

STILL LIFE

Art theory of the eighteenth and nineteenth centuries esteemed still life least in the hierarchy of pictorial themes. Still life was seen as a test of skill; a chance for the artist to show off his ability to represent objects in realistic detail. At this time, a work was valued for its subject rather than for its pure artistry. This emphasis on subject matter accounted for the success of the society painters of the rococo and the history painters of the mid-nineteenth century. Like the Dutch painters, the French Impressionists valued a work of art for its own sake, apart from its intellectual, social, or historical meaning.

Still life has had an important place in modern painting since Cézanne and the Cubists. As a result, the great period of still-life painting in the seventeenth century regained prominence in our own day. The foundations for an independent still-life tradition are found in the early Netherlandish painting of the fifteenth century. Within the context of religious art, we find small still-life arrangements of fruits, household appliances, and decorations in the backgrounds of sacred paintings. In the middle of the sixteenth century, compositions of objects gained a new importance, and eventually, the objects became larger and more prominent than the figures. The kitchen piece filled with household utensils, the market stand full of fruits and vegetables, and the butcher shop with fowl and fresh meat began to overpower the holy scenes, which continued to be the ostensible subjects of the paintings. The first truly modern still life was painted not in Holland but in Italy, by Caravaggio. Although this painting of a basket of fruit isolated against an anonymous dark background was small, the forms seem monumental. Dutch painters, adopting this scheme, brought still life to its highest development in the seventeenth century.

In the early part of the century, the still life retained a deeply symbolic meaning, in which the pessimistic spirit of Calvinism and the northern European character is recognizable. The Vanitas type of still life, filled

Jacob de Gheyn, *Sketchbook Studies of a Fieldmouse* (drawing)

with skulls and hourglasses reflecting the transitory nature of earthly things, was a popular subject. The idea of the Vanitas developed at the University of Leyden, from the theory that every item in a painting should have symbolic significance. Rotten cheese, stale bread, and wilted flowers were images of mortality.

The flower picture was an important type of still life that enjoyed great popularity in the seventeenth century and later. Its origins can be traced to the third quarter of the sixteenth century, when gardening became a popular interest in the Netherlands. Nature lovers began to want permanent inages of blossoms, familiar and exotic, to hang in their living rooms. Jan Bruegel (called "Velvet" Bruegel to distinguish him from Pieter, his famous father) painted flower arrangements with lively coloring and tapestry-like flatness that recall the careful detail of his father's peasant scenes. His *Small Bouquet of Flowers in a Ceramic Vase* (p. 116) is also really a peasant bouquet, since it assembles all the common blooms of the meadows in a botanically correct arrangement.

In "Velvet" Bruegel's work, each individual flower is painted with great realism, but, in fact, the whole is a rich fantasy. The combination of tulips and snowdrops, anemones and roses, marigolds and water lilies

Jan Bruegel, *Small Bouquet of Flowers in a Ceramic Vase*, p. 116

109

cannot have been painted from nature, because these flowers bloom at different times of the year. The individual blossoms must have been taken from independent studies and gathered imaginatively in the most beautiful bouquet possible. Once again, we find reference in this fertile bouquet to life's transitory quality. Beetles, butterflies, and insects sit like evil spirits on the leaves and flowers. Some petals have already fallen; others are about to fall. Precious stones, coins, and rings, and symbols of vanity and greed, are another part of this arrangement in dying nature. The message is that all things earthly come to an end. Death lurks behind blooming life. The light-filled, happy world is at bottom only vanity.

This tendency to moralize contrasts starkly with the joyful mood of the Italian Baroque. And in Holland, between 1630 and 1650, still life lost its element of instruction and became an expression of pleasure-seeking. There were many pictures of richly bedecked tables, a development from the kitchen pieces. Now, however, whole pictures were devoted to arrangements of bread, cheese and herring, wine and costly fruit. Lavish arrangements of precious metals, delicate crystal, and fine porcelain replaced simple kitchen tables.

The most important of the innumerable creators of these decorative breakfast and luncheon still lifes was Abraham van Beyeren, who was born in The Hague. Van Beyeren stood out among the painters of his time because of his unusual technique. He unified the whole picture with an almost impressionistic touch. Inspired by De Heem, Van Beyeren painted lavish banquet pieces of fruit, lobster, and ornate tableware, set on an expensive tablecloth. His compositions are simpler, though, and less overburdened with detail than those of De Heem.

Abraham van Beyeren,
Still Life, p. 114

The symbols of mortality typical in such still lifes were reduced in his work to a minimum. In his *Still Life* (p. 114), there are a timepiece, a flute, and some half-eaten bread, which symbolize time passing. However, our real interest is in the bright tablecloth, the sparkling lemon peel, and the iridescent reflections of light on glass and metal, all executed with the rapid movement of the paintbrush.

The late style of Dutch still life painting is represented by Jan van Huysum of Amsterdam. He was born in 1682, and most of his work was done in the eighteenth century. As his *Bouquet of Flowers in a Marble Vase*

Jan van Huysum,
*Bouquet of Flowers
in a Marble Vase*,
p. 119

(p. 119) shows, he is closer to the Rococo than to the Baroque. The finely painted petals recall the ruffles and fancy dress of his time. The relief on the vase is a play on the happy lovers picnic known as the *fête galante*. The heavy atmosphere and the proliferating and swelling plants speak the spirit of a new age, an age that ended in revolution. A detail from his still life, *Flowers and Fruit* (p. 117), shows Van Huysum's ability to

Jan van Huysum,
Flowers and Fruit,
p. 117

depict details with great realism. The leaves are three dimensional; insects and stamen are painted with fascinating objectivity. The various flowers are wonderfully realistic. There is a sultry, tropical air that is typical of Van Huysum's still lifes. Although the fruit appears fresh and appetizing, it is obviously not to be tasted in these surroundings. An evil poison seems to have overcome it. The shiny green leaves look dangerous; the orange carnation is a sickly hue; and the blue of a single flower glints against the dark background like the eye of a reptile. The buzzing insects suggest approaching decay. Still life here is truly a *nature morte*, or dead nature, the name the French began to use for still life around the middle of the eighteenth century, when Baroque vigor had begun to wane.

Most Dutch painters of still life had abandoned themselves to the purely decorative by the middle of the century. The treaty of Westphalia, concluded in 1648, ended the Thirty Years War and inaugurated a new era of peace and prosperity. The Dutch middle class, optimistic and self-confident, wanted more and more splendid still-life canvases to decorate their banquet rooms.

Flanders greatly influenced the rise of the sumptuous, decorative still life in Holland. The work of Jan Davidsz. de Heem, who spent a number of years in Antwerp, owes something to both schools. It was in Antwerp that De Heem, a Dutchman, arrived at the formula for which he is now famous: flower pieces and banquet pieces of tables overloaded with

Philips Koninck,
Mourning of Christ
(drawing)

baskets of fruit, lobster, fragile glassware, and expensive silverware. The displays were adopted from the decorative displays of Rubens' apprentices: Frans Synders, Adriaen van Utrecht, and Daniel Seghers. Jakob Rosenberg describes De Heem as one of the few Dutch painters to capture the exuberance of Flemish painting and its gorgeous color harmonies. His still lifes were often copied in the eighteenth and nineteenth centuries. A painting by Matisse is entitled *Variation on a Still Life by De Heem.*

Although there was great demand for these banquet pictures, a few Haarlem masters began to simplify their form and to concentrate on compositional structure instead of decorative effect. Their "monochrome" banquet pieces are among the most interesting and unusual works of the Dutch masters. They seem to perfect the quality of static formal abstraction found in Van Goyen's landscapes, in Vermeer's genre paintings, and in De Hooch's interiors. There is no hint of movement in these paintings, either through light or through the presence of human figures. Everything is seen in terms of pure geometrical solids and volumes, which interested these painters of the seventeenth century as they would later interest Cézanne and the Cubists. The problem of abstraction, which is the chief concern of artists of our own time, was already being explored.

Willem Claesz. Heda, *Breakfast Still Life,* p. 113

Willem Claesz. Heda was the greatest of this school. He painted still life in many rich arrangements of the same objects—dishes, crystal, a goblet. It is soon apparent that the form rather than the subject is of principal interest to him. In Heda's *Breakfast Still Life* (p. 113), there are two formal motifs: the straight line and the oval. The straight horizontal lines, like the tabletop, and the vertical lines of the glasses, construct a strong architectural framework, while the oval of the overturned goblet introduces a feeling of depth. Tension is not to be understood here in terms of movement. The geometrical form of the oval is an element of unrest, not in terms of movement, but because of its contrasting form. Heda arranges these shapes, not out of necessity or for a purpose, but out of his creative feeling for mass and form. The simplification of the composition is echoed by the reduction of colors to a ground tone, to which everything else is keyed. The yellow of the lemon is a single strong local color. The two other colors, green and brown, are seen only in broken tones or mixtures, which lie like diffuse veils over the whole picture, the brown more to the right, the green more to the left of the picture. Through the glass, we see dark reflections of the light picked up once again on the yellow lemon. This sensitive picture bears little resemblance to the rustic bouquets of Jan Bruegel.

Nevertheless, and despite all his interest in form and color, Heda remains a painter of his time, and clothes his still life in symbolism. Every object suggests the passage of time, and the end of all beauty. As a man might perceive his own nothingness at the end of his life, so the artist, at the end of this great age of painting, saw merely empty vessels, stale wine, broken glasses, and a lemon peel in the spiral form recalling a broken watch spring.

Willem Claesz. Heda, *Breakfast Still Life*

Pieter Saenredam, *Interior of St. Lawrence Church in Alkmaar*

Jan Bruegel, *Small Bouquet of Flowers in a Ceramic Vase*

Jan van Huysum, *Flowers and Fruit* (detail)

Right: Jan van Huysum, *Bouquet of Flowers in a Marble Vase*

Melchior d'Hondecoeter, *Birds*

A synthesis between Heda's sobriety and the rich decorative effect of the late still-life painters is found in Willem Kalf. Kalf lived in Paris for many years and sent back to Holland still lifes without any allegorical content. Kalf painted only appearances. He was interested in the object for its own sake, and in its possibilities for composition. The *Still Life with a Chinese Tureen* (p. 120) shows with what simple means he creates a composition. He was indebted to Heda for his economy, but his rich palette contrasted with Heda's sober colors. He employed glittering tones and the whole color scale, from lightest yellow to deep, dark red. The orange accents seen in the carpet, the ruby-colored wine, the blue of the ceramic bowl are especially rich. The Flemish liked to adorn things with such still-life elements as garlands of flowers; but the Dutch decorative sense was architectonic. For Dutchmen, still life came to symbolize the durable and the eternal, a contrast to the tumult of human life. Businessmen recuperated by contemplating the beauty of their shining possessions in orderly groupings, and as an extension of this feeling, the rich Mynheers family of Amsterdam, who emulated the life style of the Italian and French aristocracy, patronized the still-life painter Willem Kalf.

Willem Kalf, *Still Life with a Chinese Tureen,* p. 120

Among the Dutch artists specializing in still life, it was Kalf who best understood Rembrandt's legacy—realism informed and imbued with mystery. Rembrandt's example was a decisive factor in Kalf's stylistic development. Kalf combined Rembrandt's chiaroscuro technique with Vermeer's color sense and his use of controlled dots of color. The motif of the peeled lemon juxtaposed with a Delft or a Ming bowl appears often in Kalf's compositions, suggesting the artist's preference for the blue-yellow harmony favored by Vermeer. The rich Persian carpets covering the table in a Kalf painting recall Vermeer's exquisite rugs.

Like still-life painting, the painting of church interiors stressed composition. The first example of this type of painting was Jan van Eyck's famous *Madonna in the Church.* Here we have a huge Gothic inner space before us, described in the most realistic terms down to the smallest architectural detail. Here, the Madonna dominates the picture, filling two-thirds of the space of the church. In the first half of the sixteenth century, grandiose Renaissance architecture attracted Netherlandish painters, who handled it as a rich fantasy and used it to show their ability to construct one-point perspective. This is the type of scientific perspective invented in the Renaissance, in which all imaginary "lines of sight" converge in a single focus in the "true" background. This one-point perspective allowed painters to give a much more convincing sense of depth than before, because the illusion it created was consistent. The archi-

Willem Kalf, *Still Life with a Chinese Tureen*

tectural pictures of the second half of the sixteenth century are especially successful in giving an illusion of deep space. But these imaginary interiors had nothing to do with architectural truth.

The seventeenth century, with its factual spirit, had no more use for these fantastic illusionistic pictures. At the same time, the anti-mystical spirit of Calvinism divested the churches of their sense of mystery. They were no longer scenes of sacred drama.

The Haarlem master Pieter Saenredam became known as the portrait painter of church interiors. His architectural pictures are not works of the imagination, but representations of actual views. Saenredam composed in three stages. First he made a sketch on the spot. This sketch was the starting point for a construction drawing he executed with reference to the building's dimensions. The final stage was the oil painting on panel. Before painting, Saenredam may have traced the outlines of the construction drawing onto the panel. From a foundation of documentary reality, he could construct an artistic reality. Pieter Saenredam's view of the interior of the St. Lawrence Church in Alkmaar (p. 115) shows how closely this type of church interior is tied to still life, particularly in its process of abstraction. In still life, paint quality first became important for its own sake. In the architectural piece, space became important for its own sake, as the real subject of the painting. As Heda and Kalf arranged objects in relation to one another, bringing the art of composition to a new perfection, so Saenredam rèlated different types of space. Today, we know that Saenredam's architectural paintings are more than mere historical documents. We can see them as a timeless approach to the problem of pure form, so important for the abstract art of our own century. Saenredam does not allow us to see the St. Lawrence Church from any distance; he puts us directly within it. A high wall and ceiling force the glance upward toward the shadowy zone of the ceiling. The sharp vertical movement of the high columns is opposed by movement into depth created by different kinds of light, filtering through two spaces following one another. The platforms of the indented columns diminish in size as they recede backward, and the open doors also emphasize depth, which is further intensified by a system of walls, planes, and arcades running parallel to the picture plane. From these three movements—up, back, and across—the three dimensions—height, depth, and width—are created. Saenredam binds his spaces together with the glittering light that filters in through the open doors. Saenredam achieves a rare sense

Pieter Saenredam, *Interior of St. Lawrence Church in Alkmaar*, p. 115

Jacob van Ruisdael, *Interior of the Old Church in Amsterdam* (drawing)

123

of harmonious order and mystical purity, of the wholeness of a clearly
grasped reality. His architectural paintings may justly be compared with
Heda's still lifes and Vermeer's interiors.

The church pieces of Emanuel de Witte appear much richer than those
of Saenredam. De Witte was twenty years younger, and his creative
period fell within the second generation of the Golden Age. By the time
he was painting, the cool, tasteful restraint of the first generation had
been lost. In De Witte's work, the charm of the architecture painters of
the sixteenth century was united with the refreshing realism of Saenredam. De Witte's architecture was not always a copy of an existing
truth. For example, he often combined the details or the parts of very
different churches together into a visionary unity, without, however,
losing the appearance of authenticity. Reality thus became generalized.
De Witte seldom painted a topographically correct piece of architecture,

Philips Koninck,
Three Nuns (drawing)

Rembrandt, *Benjamin Departing for Egypt* (drawing)

but an impression that strikes one as generally true. In his *Choir of the New Church in Amsterdam* (p. 64), he changes the proportions to accentuate the heavenward movement. The lighting is quite arbitrary and serves to heighten the sense of the spiritual. Finally, there are the groups of figures who enliven the space. In Saenredam's architectural piece (p. 115) there are only two figures represented, whose sole purpose is to establish some relationship between the viewer and the architecture. De Witte's figures, on the other hand, are bearers of meaning. They have no quality of individuality. They are pathetically small under the high umbrella of the choir. Nameless beings, they are engulfed by the majestic stillness and greatness of the grandiose space. But they are not humiliated by their awe. They stand upright, yet without any arrogance. In them, the Calvinistic lessons of belief have awakened a devotion that encourages enjoyment in the present world. According to this belief, one pursues success and worldly well-being. The greater and the surer the success, the greater the hope of the soul of joining God in heaven. This work ethos, founded on religious principle, created a new type of man, and had more than a little to do with the economic flowering of the Netherlands.

Emanuel de Witte, *Choir of the New Church in Amsterdam*, p. 64

125

FRANS HALS

Frans Hals, *Cavalier*
(drawing)

Among the many types of paintings, portraits gave the greatest range to the Dutch love of objectivity. Artists painted many kinds of portrait, allowing themselves great interpretive freedom with their subjects. No painter used this freedom better than Frans Hals. It is surprising to note that this most Dutch of masters was not really a Dutchman. His father was a Flemish cloth manufacturer, and like so many Flemings of his time, he left for Haarlem in 1591, apparently for religious reasons. Hals was born in 1580 in Mechlin, but he grew up in Holland, where he met the artist and biographer Karel van Mander, who was also a Flemish immigrant. Van Mander had visited Italy and been influenced by the Italian masters. His art belongs to the sixteenth century in its conventionality and tendency to idealize. Hals's greatest task as a youth was to resist the influence of his teacher. His own objective was to record everyday life and to exclude everything that was foreign to his art. His great talent and his extraordinary ability to paint quickly helped him toward this goal. He was able to develop a spontaneous, personal style, which had been suggested but never quite accomplished in the work of his predecessors.

Frans Hals experienced little of the happy, carefree life that is seen in his laughing portraits. His first marriage was wretched; he allegedly received a court sentence for mistreating his wife. She died in 1615, after six miserable years with Hals. Two years later, he married again. Eleven children were born of this second marriage. He managed to support this large family until 1652, when a creditor forced him into bankruptcy. Like Rembrandt, Hals had to sell his possessions to pay his debts; but he had little to sell. The inventory of the sale lists three mattresses and bolsters, a closet, a table, and five pictures. Among these were pictures by his teacher, Van Mander.

Frans Hals, *Study*
(drawing)

Hals painted the portraits of people in their ordinary surroundings, with a sharp eye for their typical qualities, bad as well as good. But such keen observation would understandably not be treasured by his contemporaries. His tendency to exaggerate, even to caricature, brought him little sympathy. His portraits are unidealized, unbeautified documents of the time. In the group portraits and individual portraits of his twenties and thirties, the unmistakable spirit of the first generation that brought freedom to the Netherlands lives again. Those he painted in his forties and fifties celebrate the conservative outlook and desire for prosperity of a society that has arrived. Hardiness, self-satisfaction, richness of costume, and pride are found in the portraits of his sixties. They often reveal the bitterness of an old man, impoverished and ignored, who looks cynically at the society that he saw so optimistically in his early years. The middle class that he satirized no longer respected his highly original talent. He had not had a portrait commission since 1660. In 1661, the St. Luke's Guild would no longer permit him to remain a member. He had been forced to pay his debts by selling his furniture and trading paintings, among which was a portrait of Karel van Mander. Beginning in 1662, Hals received a pauper's pension of 150 guilders and three wagonloads of peat, to use as fuel. He received a commission in 1664: a group portrait of the home for the aged; but it was undoubtedly given to him out of charity rather than esteem for his talent.

Frans Hals, one of the greatest painters of his time, died, alone and poor, in the home for the aged, on August 26, 1666, and was buried in the New Church in Haarlem. Despite this bitter life, Hals's work is thoroughly good-natured. Laughter was his cure for suffering. In fact, there is hardly any painter in whose work we find so many laughing people. We find in his work all forms of laughter: the quiet smile, expressing inner happiness; the uninhibited laugh, a sign of the purest joy in life; the loose laughter of the drinker; the satisfied laughter of the cavalier; the gay laughter of children. We find other kinds as well: sarcastic laughter, mischievous and evil laughter, like the laughter of the witch Malle Babbe. This optimistic spirit belonged to Hals personally, and also to his whole epoch. His work is in many ways a mirror of his time. A good photograph can capture external reality, but Frans Hals created a spiritual truth out of the world around him through his creative vision. He was an incorruptible observer. His gaze penetrated the inner life of his subject. He gave each subject a proper estimate, without idealization. He recognized the spirit behind every façade. In a gypsy, for example, he found more warmth and goodness than in the head of the home for the aged. He saw more natural nobility in the eyes of a mulatto than in those of a distinguished burgher.

Hals recorded what he saw, without reflecting on it. He gave little importance to his own person; he seems to have left no self-portrait, which is unusual for a portrait painter. Perhaps he is the odd extra figure in one of his great paintings of rifle companies who seems to have so little in common with the others. In this face, there is no laughter, no happi-

Frans Hals, *St. Adrian's Rifle Company* (detail)

Frans Hals, *St. George's Company*

Right: Frans Hals, *Regents of the Home for the Aged* (detail)

134   Frans Hals, *Daniel van Aken*

Frans Hals, *The Gypsy*

Frans Hals, *Girl with a Basket of Fish*

ness; the gaze is disillusioned, the face puffy and weary. It is the face of a man who once had great hope, who has it no longer. His eyes pierce with their intensity. This man is not ready to reveal his feelings to us. His interest is only in others. He sees them as they really are, and not as they would like to be.

Hals received his first important commission in 1616. This was the commission for a group portrait of the St. Georges Company. These group portraits are a uniquely Dutch contribution to European painting, because they have no parallel in other countries. They could only belong to one time and one place, in which individualism had already been well established in society. The Middle Ages, too, knew the group portrait, above all in the representation of the Last Supper. But the individual had no place in such representation. Hals left not less than eight group portraits, including three regents' pieces and five shooting companies. In the latter, we see the leading members of the burgher guards who played an important role in the long fight for freedom against Spain. These paintings commemorate the time of the war. The shooting companies were more than welfare associations in case of need. In the Netherlands they date back to the Middle Ages, when Dutch burghers formed them to protect their towns against attack. In the sixteenth century, the groups began to decorate their buildings with portraits of the members. The companies became centers of social life and civic affairs. The officers in an early group portrait by Hals still show a battle-ready staunchness and a proud earnestness. A shooting company painted eleven years later, however, shows that the ambience of the companies has changed. Now, the men form a joyful, happy group who think more about eating and drinking than about war. The former revolutionary has become a secure, free burgher, out for an evening with the boys.

The figures in the *St. George's Company* (p. 130) are divided into two groups. At the left, the old officers, grouped together beside the furled flag, seem conscious of the spirit of the occasion; at the right are the young officers, led by Captain Michael de Wael, who tips his empty glass with a proud gesture and looks at us with the glassy stare of someone getting drunk. Obviously there is a gap between the two generations; they are bound together, both pictorially and spiritually, only on the stage of the group to which they belong.

Frans Hals,
St. George's Company,
p. 130

Among Hals's greatest masterpieces is the *St. Adrian's Rifle Company* (p. 129), painted in 1633. Here each member of the famous Haarlem club is seen as an individual with a unique temperament and character. The *St. Adrian's Rifle Company* offers an interesting comparison with Rembrandt's group portrait of a shooting company, *The Night Watch*. Compositionally, Hals's painting is a far more conventional work, because it emphasizes individual likenesses, treating each individual with equal importance, as was the normal tendency in the democratic group portrait. Rembrandt, on the other hand, subordinates all the figures to a single focus and a common action. Technically, on the other hand, the *St. Adrian's Rifle Company* is extremely advanced in the freedom and

Frans Hals,
*St. Adrian's Rifle
Company*, p. 129

Rembrandt,
The Night Watch,
p. 152

spontaneity of Hals's brushwork, which darts across the surface with lightning speed and brilliance. Hals paints the rich materials of elegant costumes with masterful assurance in rapid, broad strokes, which omit detail in favor of giving a realistic general impression that attempts to produce not a photographic reality, but what the eye actually sees. The composition, although it appears spontaneous and informal, has obviously been coolly calculated. Colors are reduced to a few local tones, which are broken up into many variations.

Finally, we must remark on the most exciting aspect of the work—Hals's brilliant and original painting technique, which allowed him to summarize forms in a few swift but miraculously sure strokes. In contrast to the enamelled surfaces, fine detail, and frequently reworked passages characteristic of his contemporaries, Hals's work offers us the freshness and sparkle of thick paint, visible brushstrokes, and daring highlights strategically placed to keep the picture surface lively. It is this rapid, spontaneous painting technique that gives Hals's portraits their unique quality of vitality. Painting without laborious preparatory work, he was such a master that he seldom needed to repaint an area to correct it. His virtuosity allowed him to capture the meaning of a momentary gesture and a glance. Hals's ability to record the momentary and the spontaneous made him a favorite of the Impressionist painters, who appreciated his rapid, raw painting techniques, which they later imitated.

Frans Hals, *Nicolaes Hasselaer*, p. 132

Hals's "impressionistic" painting technique is especially evident in his expressive portrait of Nicolaes Hasselaer (p. 132). The hair is waved in big curls. And one single stroke can describe a curl. The pleats of the material are similarly painted in single strokes. The modeling is determined by the way the light falls. There is no drawing in the hand either, which is made up of almost monochrome strokes of paint, laid down one after another. In the face, however, there is more care in the drawing. Here one finds sharp contrasts of tones, fine painting, reworked passages, strong modeling. But despite this, no brushstroke is overworked or unnecessary. Each is necessary to the artist's characterization of this man. The deep shadows formed by the lids, for example, add to the expression of the sitter. His eyes are intelligent and candid, but perhaps not entirely guileless. The shadows around the mouth, which lie deeper than the line of the lips, are arrogant and worldly. Sensitive nostrils, a sign of sensuality, and a narrow nose brought out by the dark shadow define the rest of the face of a man who wants to rule and to please, but who can also laugh and be charming. This man is critical but not petty, a typical example of the self-sufficient and free middle class. Nicolaes Hasselaer was Hals's most distinguished client. He lived from 1593 to 1635, and came from a distinguished old Dutch family. By the time he was thirty-three, he had already assumed the office of burgomaster of Amsterdam. All the qualities of his character that brought success and a brilliant career are seized upon by Hals in this portrait.

Frans Hals, *Daniel van Aken*, p. 134

In the portrait of Daniel van Aken (p. 134), we have a different type of person. This successful businessman does not allow himself to be posed

Frans Hals,
Study of a Head
(drawing)

in the usual clothes of the official portrait, but assumes a casual, jovial
pose, playing the violin and allowing the viewer to perceive his naïve
pride in his accomplishment. His ingenuousness, his lusty eyes and cheerful laughter make him very sympathetic to us, even though he is not
handsome. His formless nose and his thick double chin are realistically
recorded by Hals without any wish to beautify them. But they become
charming in Van Aken's winning face. As usual, Hals portrays defects
with a certain irony and humor and good feeling toward his subject.
The portrait that is known as *The Gypsy* (p. 135), belongs to a group of
genre portraits painted by Hals in his twenties, in which he could be
much freer, since he did not have to portray a specific person for a commission. To this category belong *The Happy Drinker, The Pauper, The
Laughing Cavalier*, and, finally, the painting we spoke of earlier, *Malle
Babbe*. Hals's ability to capture the moment, as in the spontaneous smile
of the *Laughing Cavalier*, is one of his most remarkable gifts. Like
numerous other genre pictures painted by Hals in the 1620's and 1630's,
this one reveals Hals's debt to Terbrugghen, who returned to Utrecht
from Rome in 1640. In Rome, Terbrugghen had been one of the many

Frans Hals,
The Gypsy, p. 135

Frans Hals,
*The Happy Drinker;
The Pauper; The
Laughing Cavalier;
Malle Babbe*, p. 88

139

painters influenced by Caravaggio, who loved large, monumental figures silhouetted against a dark background, painted from nature, with vivid colors. Hals does the same in his portrait of the *Laughing Cavalier*, but he does not experiment like Caravaggio with the contrasts produced by artificial light. Nor do his figures look stiffly posed like waxworks; instead they talk, laugh, drink, and make music in a silvery sunlight.

Frans Hals, *Girl with a Basket of Fish*, p. 136

Genre never engaged Hals, who painted only a few genre scenes. The wild hair, the provocative clothing, and the uninhibited spirit of *The Gypsy* characterize the whole life of one class of people. In the *Girl with a Basket of Fish* (p. 136), Hals goes even a step further. The three houses in the background, the sandy dunes, a stormy atmosphere, the raw sea, add to the impression of the stormy, difficult life of fishermen, who are so totally dependent on nature. In the accidental glance of the girl's eyes, we can read a whole story. As we can see in his genre pictures of women, Hals concentrates much more on the personality than on the environment.

Hals painted many portraits of women. In opposition to the vitality of the virile portraits of men, they represent passivity. Hals's women always seem conservative and cautious, without aptitude for spiritual flight. They perhaps reflect the artist's experience of two unhappy marriages and many unmarried daughters. The women painted by Hals are worthy and strong, but they lack spirit and gaiety. They convey no motherly warmth, either, although they are often quite portly. Typical of them is *The Nurse with the Child* (p. 133). Here Hals concentrates on the expensive dress and the face of the child, while the nurse, despite her attention-getting gesture, is left in the background. Despite the brilliance of his painting technique, this is a conventional portrait that lacks the insights of Hals's portraits of men. Understanding for the world of women seems absent from all his female portraits. They tend to be cool, although not unsympathetic. In his old age, lack of interest became open hate and bitter rejection. His last great commissions, done while he was on welfare, are two group portraits of the regents of the home for the aged. While he gives the male regents a certain dignity, he shows his disgust for this miserable world in the portrait of the female regents. Here we see the committee of worthy ladies, who seem the representatives of hell itself. On the table there is no money, as if all debts have been settled. The bony fingers that the chief regent lays on her knees resemble the hand of a skeleton; her tight lips and hard gaze are without mercy. The laughter that has run like a bright thread through Hals's work has now been quelled by misfortune.

Frans Hals, *The Nurse with the Child*, p. 133

Frans Hals, *Regents of the Home for the Aged*, p. 131

In this last period of his life, Hals no longer used intense pure colors. Increasingly, he harmonized dull yellowish browns and grayish blacks, and relied on chiaroscuro rather than color contrasts. Fashions had changed in Holland; bright colors in clothes were giving way to more sober hues, which may have had some influence on Hals's decision to change his color scheme, although he seems generally more dour in his old age than when he was painting gay cavaliers and gypsy girls.

Hals continued to use an impressionistic technique in his late work, constructing forms with his characteristic swift, angular strokes, but in the portrait of the lady regents, his virtuoso brushwork is visible only in the lightest passages of this essentially black and white painting. The companion portrait of the governors was painted directly onto the canvas without any underpainting, a technique adopted by Manet, a great admirer of Hals, two centuries later.

Some people believe that these two late group portraits were done out of gratitude for the funds given Hals and his wife. One reason for Hals's poverty was his unwillingness to paint elegant portraits in the style popularized by Rubens' pupil, Van Dyck. This type of portrait was in demand among the wealthier Dutch and the well-to-do all over Europe; but Hals remained the hard-drinking Bohemian painter of actuality to the bitter end. In 1666, two years after painting those haunting portraits of old age, Frans Hals died at the age of eighty-six.

Bartholomeus van der Helst,
Portrait of Pieter Potter (drawing)

JAN VERMEER

Jan Vermeer,
The Studio, p. 148;
Girl with the Pearl,
p. 145; *The Love
Letter*

Jan Vermeer was born in 1632 in Delft, and died there in 1675. It has now been 300 years since he painted his masterpieces: *The Studio*, around 1665; *Girl with the Pearl*, around 1660; and *The Love Letter*, around 1670. It has been only 100 years since this painter began to be well known. He was forgotten for 200 years, until Manet's generation rediscovered him and esteemed him among the great masters of painting. As far as themes are concerned, Vermeer's paintings belong to the genre tradition. As Dutch painting began to decline with the decline of the seventeenth century, genre painting fell into disfavor. The works of the great genre painters—De Hooch, Metsu, Steen, and Terborch—were undoubtedly treasured for their market value. But they had, for the moment, little importance for the development of painting. In his own time, Vermeer was not considered among the greatest masters of genre. His works lacked all of the usual signs activity found in this type of painting. They displayed the lovingly described interiors of De Hooch, Terborch's delight in rich materials and fine textures; but the representation of the everyday, the principal purpose of genre, is missing. Vermeer's contemporaries must have sensed that he was changing and spiritualizing the everyday world by imparting to it the sacredness of the ceremonial and the solemn. For his contemporaries, this did not seem to clarify their world, but to alienate it. They wanted the world that they loved, that they had captured in masterpieces, to be seen as it really was. They thought that life should be mirrored in art. They wanted to see their households, their native landscapes, and their neighbors with every defect and quality, but this was not Vermeer's reality. He filtered out much realistic representation of nature from his paintings. What remains is a pure expression of highest completeness and harmony. A century that had no use for form as an end in itself or for idealizing in art must have found Vermeer's idealized subjects incomprehensible, especially when they were seen in genre situations. This was probably why Vermeer fell into obscurity. Few collected his paintings, and they were little esteemed. When he was rediscovered in the nineteenth century, only fourteen authenticated works could be found, although in an inventory of 1682 there were twenty-one pictures by Vermeer. After his rediscovery, more of his work came to light, including some paintings only doubtfully attributed to him.

Vermeer was the polar opposite to Frans Hals. Between the two lies the whole expressive range of Dutch painting. Frans Hals was unchallenged master of the spontaneous impression; Vermeer was the great exponent of illuminated silence. Frans Hals painted quickly, nervously, improvising. Vermeer painted carefully, meticulously, self-consciously. Hals's world is full of sprawling life. Vermeer's world is absolutely quiet and without movement. The central theme of Hals's art is man. In Vermeer's art, it is the form of the young woman. No one could portray woman in all her goodness and completeness as Vermeer could, while no one could paint men as well as Frans Hals. In the work of these two artistic personalities, we see the whole range of the Golden Age. As contemporary geniuses they were overshadowed only by Rembrandt.

We know very little about Vermeer's life. His personal destiny is obscured behind the imporance of his work. His father was a silk weaver, picture dealer, and innkeeper. From documents, we know that Jan was baptized on October 31, 1632, in Delft, and that he married Catarina Belenes in 1653, the same year in which he entered the St. Luke's Guild, of which he was later twice president. We know that he could not live from his painting alone, probably because he was not productive enough. He died at the age of forty-three, leaving his widow with a mountain of debts and eleven children, eight of them minors. Most of his pictures found their way into the hands of his creditors, as insurance for his debts.

It is difficult to construct a chronology for Vermeer, because only two of his paintings are dated, but his stylistic development seems to cover a period of about twenty years. He was influenced first (1655—ca. 1660) by the monumental genre paintings of the Utrecht Caravaggists and then by the meticulous realism of Carel Fabritius, who also worked in Delft. Vermeer's early works, such as the *Soldier and a Laughing Girl* and the *Procuress*, emphasize story and individual figures. The works of his middle period, roughly the decade of the 1660's, such as *Woman Reading a Letter* and *The Kitchen Maid*, give more importance to space and light than to narrative or the human figure. Vermeer's palette changed, too; he abandoned the harsh chiaroscuro of Caravaggio's followers for silvery sunlight. His cool palette obviously reflected the painter's contemplative mood. During this period, Vermeer achieved the classical balance between space and the objects within it for which he is famous. It is the clarity and balance of the formal elements, and the monumental simplicity of these works, that makes them so pleasing to the modern sensibility.

Vermeer lost some of this clarity in his late works, such as *The Love Letter* of 1670. The late paintings often conceal an allegorical meaning that scholars are still trying to decipher. Perspective is exaggerated. Objects and figures are tightly integrated into an intricate, tapestry-like unity. Often light floods the background, while the figures in the foreground remain in shadow. Perhaps the most famous of Vermeer's early works are the Biblical scene *Christ in the House of Mary and Martha* (p. 147) and the raffish genre painting *The Procuress* (more politely known as *At The Tavern*; p. 150). The former is still attached to convention, despite the brilliance and sophistication of its technique; but the

Jan Vermeer, *Soldier and a Laughing Girl; The Procuress*, p. 150; *Woman Reading a Letter; The Kitchen Maid*, p. 149

Jan Vermeer, *Christ in the House of Mary and Martha*, p. 147

143

utter stillness typical of Vermeer's later works is already evident. *The Procuress*, painted in 1656, is the earliest extant painting signed and dated by Vermeer. The brothel scene it depicts was common in early northern genre painting, especially in Utrecht.

Despite the subject of *The Procuress*, there is the same sense of stillness and immobility. Through the largeness of the genre figures, the viewer is brought into proximity with what is happening. Yet he is kept at a distance by the Turkish carpet that fills up a quarter of the painting. This is a device typical of Vermeer, and found in most of his interiors. Even in his two self-portraits, we find such barriers. In the *View of Delft*, the wide canal, which we can never cross, has this function. In *A Street in Delft*, the street in the forgrund protects the house and its inhabitants from all disturbances. In *The Procuress*, the figures are separated from the viewer by the trailing tapestry.

The story in *The Procuress*, told here with a few gestures and looks, is clear. The young cavalier looks at the outstretched hand of the girl he is buying. The two onlookers smile knowingly. The girl observes the paying hand with a factual coolness, but her expression answers the action of the youth's other hand with a look of desire that echoes his expression. Her mouth is pursed into a come-hither smile, while her eyes, directed to the willingly open hand, show her desire to be paid. But the crafty expression of the old woman in the background does not change. The second cavalier confronts the viewer with a familiar grimace, as if to make him an accomplice to the transaction. Unlike the many other representations of scenes of this kind, Vermeer's *The Procuress* is not a satire or a burlesque and entirely lacks the element of the frivolous. The action is concentrated in a few gestures, which Vermeer nonetheless imbues with unmistakable meaning. These few gestures suffice to tell a whole story and to engage the viewer in the story that is portrayed. Here the young Vermeer, about twenty-four years old when he painted this picture, was still under the influence of the taste of his time, from which he could free himself only later in order to become a highly original painter.

The Kitchen Maid (p. 149), painted around 1658, two years after *The Procuress*, already shows the fully matured Vermeer. Intimacy is insured by the size of the painting, which is only 45.5 by 41 centimeters, or approximately 18 by 16 inches. *The Procuress*, on the other hand, is a large painting, measuring 143 by 130 centimeters, or approximately 56 by 51 inches. Despite its small size, *The Kitchen Maid* has great monumentality. The cool, empty room, with only a window and a small stove in the lower right, becomes adequately filled through the presence of a

Jan Vermeer, *View of Delft*, p. 61; *A Street in Delft*, p. 70

Jan Vermeer, *The Kitchen Maid*, p. 149

146   Jan Vermeer, *The Astronomer*

Jan Vermeer, *Christ in the House of Mary and Martha*

Jan Vermeer, *The Studio*

Jan Vermeer, *The Kitchen Maid* 149

Jan Vermeer, *The Procuress*

Rembrandt, *Christ and the Adulterous Woman*

single figure. The girl, who is engaged in the ordinary everyday activity of pouring milk, engages our attention through her absorption. Even though we seem close to her, with only the table between us, she remains impervious. Completely absorbed in the duties of her small world, she endows the room around her with feeling through her presence. The unity of space, objects, and person brings a sense of absolute harmony and quiet to this scene. Here there is no movement, no pathos, no sentiment, no exhibitionism, but a persisting personal vision of a timeless presence. The painting, a genre piece from its appearance, offers us an occasion to contemplate its real significance. It is a still life in the most basic sense of the term, brought by Vermeer to the highest aesthetic meaning. The golden-yellow blouse against the pale yellow wall achieves a close-valued beauty that is heightened in contrast with the blue apron. Because the colors are so nearly alike, this is a complicated relationship, well understood by the Impressionists of the nineteenth century. The outlines of the shapes stand out against the atmospheric background, giving a special breathing life to space. The objects on the green tabletop are depicted through the juxtaposition of rich touches of color that create a lively vibration. All this is unified by the pale light that fills space like a palpable substance, passing around the stationary objects in order to bring out their inner light. This light builds pale shadows, and even brings a shimmer of brightness into the darkness. In Vermeer, light becomes atmosphere, as it does in Van Goyen's landscapes. Thoré-Bürger, who rediscovered Vermeer in the nineteenth century, wrote that a naïve viewer in front of one of Vermeer's paintings wishes to see the reverse side, to find out if the wonderful light comes from an open window. We see such an open window in the painting of the *Man and Woman with Wine,* on the jacket of this book, often falsely called *The Wine Taster.* The window is only partially open, making it possible for Vermeer to mix the various types of light filtering in. Where direct daylight comes in, there is brilliant light, and colors are seen in their full tonal values. On the other hand, as light is filtered through the window shutters, it loses its intensity and becomes diffuse, allowing colors to be seen in their full intensity. Such attention to the way light changes colors was given again only by the Impressionists, whose critics railed against the unnatural colors that they used. But the blue shadows they criticized in Monet are already present 200 years earlier, in Vermeer. In his paintings, light is not only bright and shadows dark, but light and shadow have power as colors. And color photography has shown how right he and the Impressinonists were in their observation of the influence of light on color, and how lacking in objectivity our eyes often are in terms of discerning colors, especially when they are transformed by the reflection of light. The painting of the *Man and Woman with Wine* was apparently done around 1660. By this time, Vermeer had already painted a whole series of similar genre scenes, which, in opposition to *The Kitchen Maid,* were richer in composition and execution. After the reduction of genre to a pure representation, he returned to themes that told a story. But Ver-

Jan Vermeer, *Man and Woman with Wine,* book jacket

153

Nicolaes Maes, *Woman Spinning* (drawing)

meer's lack of interest in storytelling shows itself in the arrangement of the elements like a still life. This is particularly noticeable in *The Procuress*. In the *Man and Woman with Wine*, the action comes to a standstill, as if by magic. All movement is crystallized in a shimmer of light and color. The two people are locked in space as in a glass bell. Man has become a thing among things. This painting must be placed among the many scenes of cavaliers and maidens popular at the time. Wine and music often are present in these paintings, since they were thought of as the attributes of the courtesan. Yet Vermeer is remote from the obvious meaning of *The Procuress*. This classical representation is profoundly different from the many tavern and bordello scenes of his contemporaries. Among his many pictures of women engaged in their household tasks, alone or with a cavalier, there is only one example by Vermeer that may have been a portrait, the famous *Girl with the Pearl* (p. 145). It was auctioned off in 1882, long after the rediscovery of Vermeer, for 2¹/₂ guilders. Today it is the greatest attraction at the Mauritshuis in The Hague. We see here only a detail of the suggested portrait (which lacks

Jan Vermeer,
Girl with a Pearl,
p. 145

154

the whole background of the yellow wall against which the bright blue head-kerchief is silhouetted, and the silent dark wall adjoining it, before which the exquisitely modeled face raises itself so eloquently). It is a face full of surprise and question, the face of a child filled with the melancholy of foresight, but still clear and innocent. The eyes lock with those of the viewer. The girl is complete, withdrawn into herself. The matte softness of her skin, the rosy lips, and the rich oval of her face areas, areas complete and perfect as the pearl in her ear. The double color chord of yellow and blue, familiar to us from *The Kitchen Maid*, is elaborated here to become a three-color chord of yellow, blue, and rosy red in the lips. The dark background, unusual for Vermeer, surrounds the girl's head, and becomes a deep, mysterious shadow, from which the face appears. The light-dark contrast, which in Rembrandt is an expression of spirituality, is used by Vermeer in the service of a pure, painterly vision.

Vermeer's most complete and most famous painting, *The Studio* (p. 148), which is considered his masterpiece, has two signatures: one false, by a later hand, signed Pieter de Hooch; and the other, the genuine signature of Jan Vermeer. The two signatures lead us to conclude that Pieter de Hooch was more esteemed than Vermeer, since the false signature was doubtless affixed in order to demand a higher price for the painting.

Jan Vermeer, *The Studio*, p. 148

There has been much speculation about the meaning of this painting. Most people wish to see in the girl in blue, Clio, the muse of history. (The presence of the map of Holland, in the background, seems to support this theory.) Others see here the allegory of fame with her laurel wreath and trumpet. Still others believe that the painter is Vermeer himself, and that the girl is his daughter. But whatever one's theory, the allegorical or autobiographical meaning is obviously an afterthought, which is secondary to the transcendent quality of the paint itself. Like all of Vermeer's spaces, the studio has only scanty depth. In the foreground, we find again a drapery that keeps the viewer at a distance from the figures in the painting and also cuts off the light source. Behind the drapery, a magical world is opened before us. There is no action, only timeless presences, halted like the girl in her peaceful innocence and quiet patience. It is a view of unchanging beauty, which suggests that time has held its breath in order to preserve this moment for eternity.

Everything in this sensitive scene is quiet, for the smallest movement could destroy the magic of the moment. All the details of the everyday here take on a special meaning, and the colors, bathed in soft light, seem to suggest a remarkable time of the day, unlike any hour we know.

In this work, Dutch painting arrived at its classical high point—classical in Johann Winckelmann's sense of "eternal simplicity and still grandeur." Vermeer, as Friedländer says, rises above the great number of genre painters like a "humming bird among sparrows." The most important types of picture for which the Golden Age is known, genre and still life, are bound together in Vermeer's timeless work.

REMBRANDT

The least typical practitioner of Dutch painting was the greatest. We are speaking, of course, of Rembrandt. His work came from his own experience and feelings; it had little connection with the political, social, or economic issues of his time. Although he was involved with banal, everyday problems, his works transcended their commonplace subjects to become the highest art. Rembrandt's art was animated neither by the spirit of the times nor by the taste of the times but by a totally personal impulse. Although he never intended to stand apart from society, Rembrandt found himself isolated by his superior gifts as an artist and his sensitivity as a human being. This isolation was often a source of bitterness in Rembrandt's life. Rembrandt was no neurotic outsider: He lived life fully; he liked company, wine, and women; he was neither a saint nor a cynical man-hater; but he *was* a genius. He was preoccupied with his art in a way that placed him at a distance from ordinary affairs. Rembrandt's paintings surpass those of his contemporaries, not only for their artistry, but because of their understanding and sympathy. Today, 300 years after Rembrandt painted, we see him as the great individualist of art history. More than Michelangelo and Leonardo da Vinci, more than Dürer and Grünewald, he demonstrated independence from the taste of his age. At the same time, he was the artist in whose work all of the characteristics of his age found the greatest synthesis. Rembrandt was undeniably an artist of his century, despite the individuality and time-lessness of his creation.

Rembrandt was no specialist like his contemporaries, including even Vermeer and Hals. By refusing to specialize, he showed his independence from the common practice of his times. Instead, he painted every kind of picture. He glorified the portrait in all of its forms: individual portrait, double portrait, group portrait, as well as genre, still life, and landscape. He handled historical themes, mythological themes, and Old and New Testament stories; and his mastery of the etcher's needle and engraver's tool was as great as his mastery of the paintbrush. He was, in other words, a universalist. He saw Holland's destiny as greater than that of a small European country. He entered into the Jewish world, into the Biblical world, into the world of the tragic and the dark, and found meaning in all of them. All worlds were part of his great universal creation: the Bible, history, mythology, his own environment. All live again in his work with convincing reality.

Rembrandt's work can best be understood in relation to his personal development. Born Rembrandt Harmensz. van Rijn on July 15, 1606, in Leyden, he belonged to the second generation of artists that grew up after the liberation of Holland, and thus stood between Frans Hals and Vermeer. His father was a miller, and the mill on the Oude Rijn River outside Leyden gave the family its name. His mother was the daughter of a baker. But the economic connections of his parents must have been good, since they were able to decide that Rembrandt, the second youngest of their seven children, was to be trained as a scholar. He was to be educated according to the schedule set down by the Humanist Erasmus of Rotterdam: after seven years of childhood, seven years of Latin school and seven years of university. So, in 1620, at the age of fourteen, Rembrandt left the Latin school in Leyden in order to enter the famous university there. He did not stay long. His first biographer, the Leyden Burgomaster Olfers, reports he had a natural aptitude for drawing and painting, which finally convinced his parents to send him, against his own wishes, to study art with a painter. His Latin school and university education were nevertheless important for Rembrandt's development as an artist, because they brought him into contact with antiquity and with the Old and New Testaments.

For three years, the young student studied with the distinguished painter Jacob Isaacsz. van Swanenburgh in Leyden, where he learned not much more than the rudiments of painting technique. Next, he spent six months with Pieter Lastman in Amsterdam. These months were far more important for his artistic development. Lastman had spent three years in Rome, where he came into direct contact with the great masters of the Italian early Baroque: the Caracci, Caravaggio, and the German Elsheimer, who also worked in Rome. Through Lastman, Rembrandt was brought into contact with Dutch history painting, a type of work using conventional themes that had regained popularity through the new interest in light and dark contrasts, called chiaroscuro. Rembrandt did not use Caravaggio's tricks of theatrical lighting. He introduced light to animate an indefinable hollow space with a mysterious quality that suggested the artist's perception of the mystery of life itself.

Rembrandt's first history painting immediately attracted attention in Leyden, and soon he was receiving portrait commissions. His reputation quickly spread to Amsterdam, where he moved in 1631 in the hope of attracting lucrative commissions. In a short time, he was the most sought after among portrait painters by the rich burghers in the town. At the age of twenty-six, he received his first major commission, *The Anatomy Lesson of Dr. Tulp*, a work that made him famous throughout Holland.

The Baroque interest in the subject of anatomy, which had been discovered by the Humanists during the Renaissance, was related to the favorite Calvinist theme, the Vanitas. Rembrandt's painting was a rather macabre version of the Vanitas theme, and it was a sensation. In the foreground, we find not the members of the surgeons' guild, whose portraits were the subject of the painting, but—illuminated in a flaring light—the body of the corpse undergoing dissection, on whom the eyes of the viewer as well as those of the doctors are fixed. Because of this focus, which is both visual and psychological, the work has a high dramatic climax that ordinary group portraits lack. (One may compare *The Anatomy Lesson*, for example, with Hals's *St. George's Company*, painted five years earlier; the latter, although full of vitality, has no such dramatic climax.) The realism with which Rembrandt described the details of the corpse dissection was a sign of extraordinary daring, even considering the taste of the time for realism. Finally, we must note the light that comes from a single source, with an air of mystery and magic, to express the illuminating power of knowledge.

Rembrandt,
*The Blinding of
Samson*, p. 162

Rembrandt's work during his thirties exhibits an extraordinary sense of pathos and drama—quite unlike the Dutch taste for the intimate and contemplative. At this time, Rembrandt was nearer to the Italian and Flemish Baroque than to the art of his native land. One of the greatest works of this period was *The Blinding of Samson* (p. 162). Here Samson's blinding is shown with gruesome brutality. We are witnessing the death struggle of a titan, who fights against the overwhelming strength of his enemies. All movement in the composition converges on the pain-wracked face of Samson: the diagonal of the halberd, the line going through the helmets of the soldiers, and, above all, the line going from the two outstretched arms of Delila to Samson's clenched fist focus our attention on the blinded hero. They are intensified through the rich swell of harsh light in the background that illuminates the horrible scene from behind. Then there is the fleeing Delila, who holds Samson's shorn locks, casting back a glance of triumphant hatred at her victim.

The model for Delila was a woman who would have the greatest meaning for Rembrandt's life and work: Saskia van Uylenburgh. Rembrandt met her in the house of an art dealer, where he had lived for some time. She was the daughter of a well-to-do burgomaster, and was pretty and extravagant, a combination pleasing to both Rembrandt the artist and Rembrandt the man. Many times before the two were married in 1634, Saskia posed for him as a model. Her rich dowry, her social position, and his artistic success accelerated the painter's social rise. The few years that they spent together were the happiest and most carefree of Rembrandt's life. They lived so extravagantly that the young married couple were rumored to be squandering the Uylenburghs' dowry with ostentation. Doubtless there was some truth to these rumors, but for Rembrandt these were years of untroubled joy, before his fortune fell. His attitude, in bad times as in good, was the same independence of convention and the taste of the time.

Rembrandt, *Saskia
with her Child* (drawing)

The peak of his artistic and social success was the commission for a
group portrait of the eighteen members of the Amsterdam shooting club
headed by Captain Frans Banning Cocq. The result was Rembrandt's
largest painting, which also became his most controversial. The actual
title of this work is *The Company of Captain Frans Banning Cocq and
Lieutenant Willem van Ruytenburch*, but the picture became known
popularly as *The Night Watch*. That the scene took place during the day
was not discovered until after the World War II, when the picture was
removed from its wartime hiding place and cleaned. When the dark
varnish was removed, it was obvious that, despite the strong light-dark
contrasts in the painting, Captain Banning Cocq was calling his reserve
company to arms by daylight. As in *The Anatomy Lesson of Dr. Tulp*,
the sharpest contrasts exist between the two main figures, the captain

Rembrandt,
The Night Watch,
p. 152

and the lieutenant. These two figures are also the source for the tonal contrasts that unify the painting: the lemon yellow of the lieutenant's brilliant uniform is repeated in the dress of the little girl in the crowd, and the red of the captain's sash is seen again in the figures of the men holding guns on the left and in the costume of the drummer on the right. The yellow-red harmony, with its warm glow, was a favorite of Rembrandt's, and appears again in his late work.

Individual figures in this painting move in opposing directions. Their movement can be diagrammed as a zig-zag that leads the eye back and forth in space, weaving in and out of the successive planes of the picture. One writer on Rembrandt, Jacob Rosenberg, has identified four points: the glove of the captain establishing the picture plane; the foot of the running boy on the right, the second plane; the figure of the mysterious little girl, the third; and the standard-bearer behind her, the background plane.

The strange figure of the girl has been interpreted in several ways, as the Queen of Sports, for instance, with a game bird hanging from her belt. We know that the occasion is a festive one. The company fool wears oak leaves in his helmet, and a dwarf has a dunce cap and bells. The little girl carries a silver trophy, presumably for the winner of the shooting contest. Some interpreters have seen her as a dream image of Rembrandt's wife, Saskia, who died the year that *The Night Watch* was painted. There is something ghostly and supernatural in the strange light that falls on her.

Every detail in *The Night Watch* is carefully worked out so that the composition has not only exciting movement, but stable balance as well. The architecture in the background is divided into three parts, so that the advancing figures in the center are separated from the groups on the right and the left, which balance each other.

Because each of the members of the company had to pay a share of Rembrandt's commission, they were particularly interested in their own individual portraits. Usually, artists who painted group portraits gave equal attention to each of the sitters, but Rembrandt was unable to compromise artistic truth in order to please his patrons; that would never allow for the unified effect he wished to create. So he subordinated the individual faces and their details to the whole. Catching the company in a moment of dramatic activity, he pictures them preparing to march, not formally grouped together, posing for their portraits. Because of this, the huge painting looks like only a part of a larger work. Needless to say,

Rembrandt, *Landscape with the Baptism of the Treasurer*

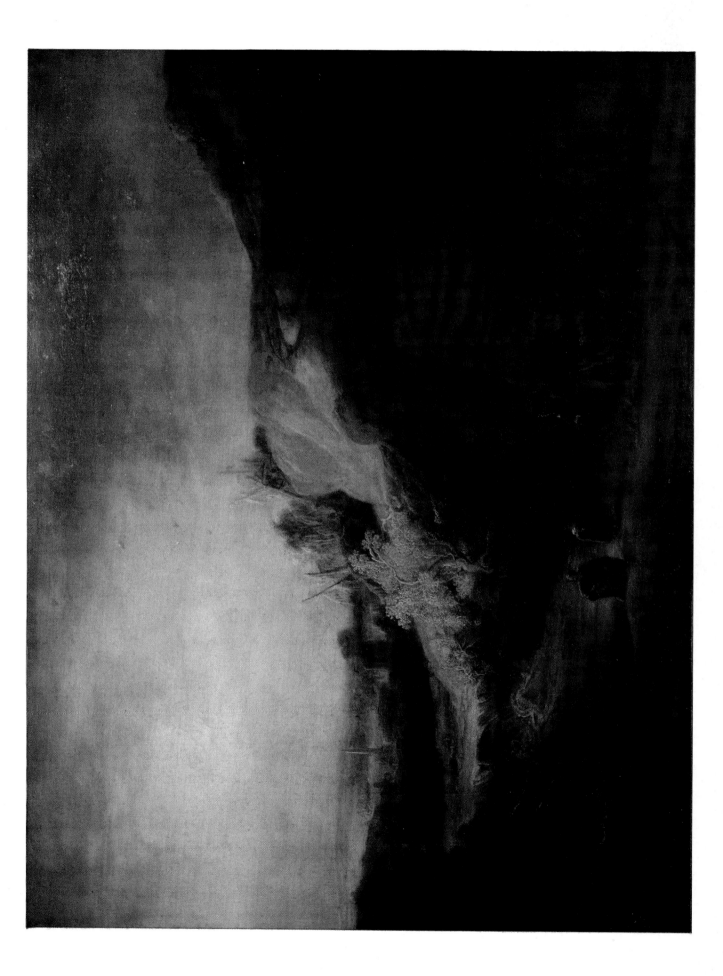

Rembrandt, *The Blinding of Samson*

Rembrandt, *The Blessing of Jacob*

Rembrandt, *The Jewish Bride*

Rembrandt, *Braunschweig Family Group*

Rembrandt, *Portrait of Hendrickje Stoffels*

168   Rembrandt, *Self-Portrait as the Apostle Paul* (detail)

the company was not happy with Rembrandt's work. In a detail of *The Night Watch* (p. 152) we see the principal group on which the painting's whole movement depends: "The young Lord Purmmerland (Banning Cocq) gives as captain the command to his lieutenant, Lord Vlardinger (Willem van Ruytenburgh), to call the company to arms." Thus wrote the captain of the guard next to a copy of the painting that he had made for a family album. This is a lusty drinking and eating company, something like the company of officers painted by Frans Hals; these are energetic men of action, who are ready to fight for their homeland. Here again is the militant spirit of the first generation, who remember their battle for independence. *The Night Watch* is a memorial to the great fighting spirit of the Dutch people, a fact that was later recognized. In 1885, when *The Night Watch* was hung in its place of honor in the new Rijksmuseum in Amsterdam, the fourteen attendants who carried in the enormous painting spontaneously began to sing the Dutch national anthem.

In these years of the 1630's, Rembrandt also discovered the landscape. It is surprising how late he developed his deepest feeling for nature. Apparently, his universalizing spirit found the native landscape too specific, too intimate, too special. Paintings of men and history, on the other hand, gave him more possibilities to express his whole personality. The landscapes painted during Rembrandt's thirties were really only preparations for the landscape etchings of his forties, in which he arrived at the classical simplicity of his late style. The landscapes painted during the years with Saskia are merely topographical renderings of cypresses and oaks, Dutch windmills and Roman temple ruins, obelisks and picturesque peasant houses, all thrown together in a fairy-tale-like setting. Old memories of his study with Lastman caused him to mix echoes of colorful Venetian painting with his own realistic sketches. What binds these elements together despite their differences is the relationship of the forces of nature, that which transpires between heaven and earth. Storms whistling through trees, the rainy battle of light with heavy masses of clouds, the wild turbulence of water, and, above all, the magic of a mild, light afternoon sun—we see these elements in his late as well as in his early landscapes.

The *Landscape with the Baptism of the Treasurer* (p. 161) shows the obvious influence of Hercules Seghers. The clump of bushes pushed up close to the picture plane, the diffuse atmosphere, the pure tonal painting, and finally the dramatic chiaroscuro—all of these exist in Rembrandt's earlier work, but he has given them a new spirit in the strength of his expression and simplification of form. In details, Seghers remains clear and distinct, even in the shadows and misty distances, but Rembrandt now depicts only massive forms, the basis of landscape structure, boldly modeled through light and shadow. Now only the details essential to the composition are emphasized: the gnarled oak trees, through whose leaves light vibrates. The figures, while quite detailed, remain lost in vague shadows. The transition from sky to earth, which Seghers represents with

Rembrandt,
Landscape with the Baptism of the Treasurer, p. 161

169

a clear horizon line, remains ambiguous in Rembrandt. The clouds, drifting earthward, bind land and atmosphere into an inseparable unity and create a mysterious, evocative mood.

We can hardly see this as a mere play between light and shadow. It is rather a magical conflict between the forces of nature—the powers of heaven and earth—a dramatic, symbolical equivalent to the baptism of the Ethiopian by the Apostle Philip, which is the subject of the painting. Rembrandt expresses himself completely, foreshadowing what he will later become. Jacob van Ruisdael's art would be unthinkable without these landscapes of Rembrandt's, upon which he based his life's work; while for Rembrandt, the paintings remain merely a transitional step in his development.

The crucial year for Rembrandt, both as an artist and as a man, was 1642. In that year, he finished *The Night Watch,* and in that same year, Saskia died. With Saskia's death, Rembrandt bade farewell to the happy times of his youth. The following years were the most difficult and strife-torn of his life. To the pain of losing his beloved wife was added the burden of economic worries. The extravagant life that he had led with Saskia had brought him to the brink of ruin. The unfavorable reception of *The Night Watch* did not help matters. Embittered, Rembrandt withdrew from society behind the closed doors of his own household. His only friend in these hard times was his son Titus, the only child who survived of the four Saskia had borne him.

Titus was cared for by Geertje Dircx, the widow of a trumpeter, who is familiar to us through two drawings Rembrandt made of her. In these drawings we see her as a person of little intelligence, an aging woman with a sunken, stupid expression. Despite this, Rembrandt maintained alliance with her until 1649, when, after many quarrels, she brought a lawsuit against him. The records of this affair reveal Geertje as a hysterical and stubborn woman. We can imagine how miserable Rembrandt must have been with her.

Not long before the lawsuit, a woman entered his household with whom Rembrandt would live until her death. In 1645, Geertje engaged the teen-aged Hendrickje Stoffels as a maid. The sympathy Hendrickje showed Rembrandt soon bound the lonely forty-year-old painter to this young girl of humble origin. Although Rembrandt wished to make her his second wife, he was kept from legalizing their relationship by the terms of Saskia's will, which set forth that Rembrandt would lose Saskia's estate if he should ever remarry. One can easily imagine how difficult this illegitimate relationship made Rembrandt's life, especially in puritanical, Calvinist Holland. But the tragedy of his personal life had no adverse effect on his work. On the contrary, it was only now, despite unhappiness and suffering, that he found his true destiny and was at last able to unite the two elements in his work: the lofty Baroque spirit and the down-to-earth bourgeois.

A comparison of *The Night Watch* with *Christ and the Adulterous Woman* (p. 151), painted two years later, reveals how much Rembrandt

Rembrandt, *Landscape* (drawing)

had developed artistically during such a short time. In the latter, restlessness and disquiet is transformed into heroic pathos, and movement is created without diminishing the dramatic impact. The form of expression follows from the inner meaning of the scene. In order to grasp the message properly, one must refer to the Biblical text Rembrandt is illustrating. In Rembrandt's representation, the various episodes of the story are told simultaneously. "She stood in the middle" is expressed by the woman being placed in the exact center of the composition. "What do you say?" is expressed through the Pharisee's outstretched hand. Christ's anticipation is expressed in the stillness of his figure. The final heavenly forgiveness pours in as a ray of light. Every gesture is important and expresses the meaning of the Biblical text. Rembrandt has followed the Biblical text faithfully, yet has brought the scene to life. With dramatically focused light, he has created a powerful artistic effect—particularly in the glittering gold altar that emerges from the darkness behind the kneel-

171

ing woman. Contours and colors are masterfully broken by shadows, and a memorable image is created by the rich artistry of this work, which unites visual and emotional meaning.

Rembrandt, *Christ and the Adulterous Woman*, p. 151

The composition of *Christ and the Adulterous Woman* should be compared with that of *The Night Watch*. In the former, horizontal and vertical lines are dominant; the only diagonal (running from Christ's hand to the Pharisee's to the adulteress) is not strongly accented, and it is quickly lost in the swinging end of the woman's garment. The principal figures—strung out in *The Night Watch*, as well as in *The Blinding of Samson*, across the lower range of the picture—are here seen in the middle ground, behind a wide zone of shadows; they have no relationship to any reality outside of the painting. The painting belongs to the period in Rembrandt's career that has been called his "solemn style."

The first years of Rembrandt's life with Hendrickje and Titus were generally harmonious, but unhappiness plagued the family. Hendrickje was expecting a child, and an "observant" neighbor reported this develop-

Rembrandt, *Titus' Nurse* (drawing)

ment to the church elders. Both were censured, and Hendrickje was forbidden to take Communion. This misfortune caused Rembrandt to lose what social standing he had left. The result was that his numerous creditors, who had kept still until this time, began to demand their money, descending on him like a pack of wolves. For two years, he kept them at bay, but in 1656, the court ruled that he had to sell his possessions in order to pay them off. Rembrandt's debts were about 8,000 guilders. His house was evaluated at 11,000 guilders, but it brought less than half of that at auction, because his creditors conspired to keep the bidding low. Rembrandt was still in debt, although he had sold everything. Fortunately, Hendrickje and Titus were clever enough to devise a way for the poverty-stricken Rembrandt to continue working. In 1658, they set themselves up as art dealers, and in December, 1660, they signed a contract with Rembrandt, whereby he gave them all of his paintings in return for food and lodging. By becoming an employee of his own family, Rembrandt was able to outwit his creditors.

To society, Rembrandt was dead, but this did not prevent him from painting. He painted some of his greatest works during these sad years. Even greater misfortunes were to follow. In 1662, Hendrickje died; six years later, Titus, too, was dead. In his last years, Rembrandt was cared for by his daughter Cornelia, Hendrickje's child, who was born in 1654. On October 4, 1669, Rembrandt died, at the age of sixty-three. He was buried in the Westerkerk in Amsterdam.

In his old age, Rembrandt concentrated on themes from the Old Testament. Now he was no longer interested in the bloody and dramatic events of the Bible that he had depicted in his youth, but in such profound, still themes as *David Playing the Harp Before Saul, Haman in Disgrace, The Return of the Prodigal Son,* or *The Blessing of Jacob.* He would concentrate on a detail of the scene and bring the figures forward to fill the frame. The boundaries here have disappeared; man is seen openly and nakedly in his suffering, in his happiness, in his humiliation.

The Jewish Bride (p. 164) — a name given to the painting in the nineteenth century — cannot be considered one of these Old Testament subjects, since contemporary documents reveal that it is the marriage portrait of an actual couple. The typical Jewish betrothal gesture of Rembrandt's time, which binds the two together, gives the painting its timeless quality. Here we see the whole of the late Rembrandt. In the guise of a real couple, we see the Biblical Jacob and Rachel, Boas and Ruth, or Tobias and Sarah, or perhaps even Titus and his bride, Magdalena van Loo. With all of these possible associations, the painting becomes the spiritual symbol of earthly love, of the love between man and woman. In its multiple and complex meaning, love is here seen as attachment in its true sense, that is, as man is attached to the woman who belongs to him. Love means here protection and security, symbolized by the way the man places his hand over the heart of his bride, offering her his protection. Love here is true, quiet, strong; love is understanding without words, without glances; it exists in simply being near the beloved.

Rembrandt, *David Playing the Harp Before Saul; Haman in Disgrace; The Return of the Prodigal Son; The Blessing of Jacob,* p. 163
Rembrandt, *The Jewish Bride,* p. 164

173

Love also means here illumination through beauty. In order to express this, Rembrandt has enriched his palette with royal extravagance. Mellow gold and deep red shine forth through streaming light. Even the shadows are burnished with rich golden-brown tones. The red seems to glow with an inner warmth, like the inner spirituality of the woman. *The Jewish Bride*—painted four years before Rembrandt's death—issues from the spiritual depths of its creator, who, despite bitter reversals and a difficult fate in life, was able to capture for all time the highest offering of heavenly grace.

Rembrandt, *Braunschweig Family Group*, p. 165

A study of Rembrandt should conclude with some remarks about the kind of painting that brought him fame as a young artist—the group portrait. He received the commission for the *Braunschweig Family Group* (p. 165) a year before his death. Between this painting and *The Anatomy Lesson of Dr. Tulp* are thirty-six years, more than a generation. In this period of time, the whole of Rembrandt's artistic development is encompassed, from the vehement vitality of his early style to the enlightened profundity of his late works. Here the family group has come to rest. Man, freed from the burden of his public tasks and outside responsibilities, returns to the intimate space of the home, where he is seen as he is, without pathos, without worldly ambition. As *The Jewish Bride* is a timeless portrait of lovers, so this painting stands as a perennial image of the family. The mother with her child on her lap—a pose borrowed from the Madonna and Child—is an enduring figure of motherly love. The father, a bit withdrawn, but linked to the family in the pose of his body, is truly the head of the house, on whom the whole family depends and leans. In contrast to this scene full of inner order and harmony is the energetic painting technique, which gives the impression of a happy freedom of execution. The pigment is laid on in thick clumps, creating nervous vague contours, and wide, churned-up planes, which suddenly change and become quiet. Rembrandt's technique was quite distinct from the taste of his time, which preferred smooth strokes and polished surfaces. Rembrandt sets down his brushstrokes with a force that makes his modeling seem almost like that of a sculptor. In fact, it was once remarked that the colors of his paintings are so thickly laid down that one feels as if one could take hold of them. Another observer once noted his "careless execution," to which Rembrandt is supposed to have answered, "A work is finished when the artist can recognize his own portrait in it."

Rembrandt did not need public approval; he worked for himself alone. For the first time in the history of art, we have a painter who is a fully autonomous personality, working only out of inner need, the way that the modern painter works. His self-portraits have nothing in common with the ordinary Dutch self-portrait; they are pure records of inner states. Free from any idealizing or reflection, they show us that Rembrandt's artistic truthfulness extended even to his own person.

In his youthful portraits, we see Rembrandt as a carefree extrovert. He is small, slightly plump, with an open, even slightly vulgar face dominated by a bulbous nose and a broad mouth. In a portrait of Rembrandt

Rembrandt,
Hendrickje Sleeping
(drawing)

with Saskia, we see in his expression a gaiety and perhaps too great an appetite for the common and the everyday. The self-portraits done after Saskia's death show a critical, prematurely aged man, who is turned completely inward. In the late portraits, the face becomes even more pinched, the eyes more piercing, the expression harsher and more critical. But it is clear that Rembrandt is judging himself. The last self-portrait was done only a few months before his death. All the bitterness has disappeared; heavy shadows rising from below cover the face like a dark veil; but the eyes are illuminated by peace and contentment, as if a lifelong battle has at last come to a close.

In the Rijksmuseum in Amsterdam there is a self-portrait, in which Rembrandt has painted himself as the Apostle Paul (p. 168). Such masquerades were common with Rembrandt. It is interesting that he identified himself at this time—the picture was painted in 1661—with the strife-torn Apostle

Rembrandt,
*Self-Portrait as the
Apostle Paul,* p. 168

175

Rembrandt, *Christ Carrying the Cross* (drawing)

who was called by God. It may be taken as a sign of the artist's unswerving confidence in himself and his creations. As Paul took up the mission of his calling, so Rembrandt was true to his own difficult vocation, which finally forced him to stand outside of fashion and society in order to express more profound spiritual truths. Identifying himself with St. Paul, Rembrandt implies a belief that he was divinely chosen for a special destiny among men.

With Rembrandt's exalted late paintings, the Golden Age of Dutch painting comes to a close. As St. Paul, the aged painter stares at us with a pained, questioning look. His sadness, we might suppose, is the tragedy of old age, which has seen the passage of all earthly pleasures and beauty. The understanding expression on Rembrandt's wrinkled face, however, reassures us that, at least in the greatest art, this passage is halted, and time stands still.

GLOSSARY

abstraction

A painting composed of line, color, planes, and volumes organized in a design that has connection with actual objects or scenes.

aerial (atmospheric) perspective

Perspective in which objects are made to appear near to the viewer by being pictured in sharp detail, and objects are made to recede by being painted in blurred outline (or in a blurred atmosphere)* and cool colors.

architectonic

A quality in painting or sculpture relating to the structural qualities found in architecture that emphasize horizontal and vertical elements.

Baroque

An energetic style in the history of art that employed free technique, diagonal movement, opposing masses, and vigorous study of possible contrasts in spatial areas and color tones. The Baroque period extended from about the beginning of the seventeenth century until well into the eighteenth century.

chiaroscuro

Strong contrasts of shadow and light employed to create drama and movement in a painting and to model forms.

continuous space

Space that is unified through light and atmosphere, rather than separated into distinct foreground, middle ground, and background.

cool colors

Blue, green, and violet; their respective opposites on the color spectrum are the warm colors—orange, red, and yellow.

Cubism

Early-twentieth-century movement in painting whose exponents created pictures showing interrelationships of geometric forms and structural planes.

Expressionism

A method of creating a work of art, in which the artist presents his subject in subjective, emotional terms rather than in factual, objective terms.

genre

Painting of subjects connected with the ordinary activities of everyday life.

history painting

Painting whose subject is derived from historical or Biblical events, or from events described in the ancient classics. From about the fifteenth to the nineteenth century, this type of painting was regarded more highly than any other kind.

horizon line

In a landscape painting, the point at which the ground and sky appear to come together. The "vanishing point" on the horizon line is the meeting point of parallel lines used to establish perspective.

Italianate

Having qualities or aspects relating to Italian influence.

linear perspective

Perspective employing a horizon line and one or more vanishing points, toward which parallel lines are drawn to create the illusion of depth or recession into the distance.

Mannerism

An art style that existed during most of the sixteenth century. It often involved distortion—such as the elongation of the human figure by El Greco — exaggeration in color and movement of line, and off-balance picture composition.

nature morte

The French term for "still life," especially after treatment of such subject matter lost its liveliness around the beginning of the eighteenth century.

nervous line

A line in a drawing or painting that, during its progression, changes width or direction to express underlying tension or emotion.

one-point perspective

Perspective used to create space that has only one vanishing point. More complicated forms of perspective involve several vanishing points.

painterly

A quality in a work of art in which the paint itself — and its application — is the medium through which the artist expresses his feeling. Characteristics include blurred outlines, visible brush strokes, and summary "impressionistic" paint application wherein one stroke does the work of many.

picture plane

The flat picture surface within which the artist starts to create his pictorial illusion.

rococo

An airy, busy, often asymmetrically balanced style of painting and design that used many curves and frivolous devices. Rococo style existed in Europe in the mid-eighteenth century.

still life

Paintings of flowers, fruits, vegetables, or kitchen utensils arranged on a tabletop or other flat surface.

Surrealist

An artist who expresses his subject on canvas, in literature, or on film as if it were in a dream, and who includes objects representing dream symbols.

tableaux de mode

Genre paintings whose subject is upper-middle-class manners and mores.

tension

Effect obtained in a picture composition that has been devised to compel the eye to move from one point of reference to an opposing point of reference or in which the figures seem cramped within the space depicted.

tonal painting

A method of creating on canvas the illusion of a form by the juxtaposition of dark, medium, and light tones of color. Tonal painting is created with contrasts of light and dark values rather than contrasts of color.

Vanitas still life

A still-life arrangement in which such objects as faded flowers, hourglasses, mirrors, and skulls are employed to point out life's ultimate vanity.

Avercamp, Hendrick
Amsterdam 1585–*ca.* 1636

He was a renowned Dutch landscape painter of the early period of the Golden Age. Typical of his work are his winter scenes containing small-sized human figures in multicolored dress. He reveals stylistic ties with Willem Buytewech and Esaias van de Velde. His nephew and pupil, Barent Avercamp, is less highly regarded and achieves stylistic independence only in his later works. Hendrick Avercamp's winter scenes were imitated, with variations, by Jan van Goyen, Aert van der Neer, Aelbert Cuyp, and Jan van de Capelle.

Text: pp. 46–47
Picture: p. 36
His chief works are in Amsterdam, Rotterdam, London, Cologne, and The Hague.

Backhuysen, Ludolf
Emden 1631–1708 Amsterdam

This seascape painter learned the fine points of painting from Allaert van Everdingen. Although his work does not measure up to that of Willem van de Velde the Younger, he is one of the best Dutch marine painters and sketchers. His craft led him to England, where he lived for a number of years, where his work was highly praised, and where he earned a great deal of money by making copies and variations of his own pictures and sketches. He returned to Amsterdam in his later years.

His chief works are in Amsterdam, London, Dresden, Paris, Berlin, Vienna, and Munich.

Berchem, Nicolaes
Haarlem 1620–1683 Amsterdam

A skilled and versatile painter and sketcher, Berchem worked mainly in Amsterdam. His pastoral landscape with herds of grazing cattle are well known and reveal an Italian influence; but he also did winter scenes and depicted Biblical and mythological themes. Landscapes similar to Berchem's were depicted by Jan Both and Adam Pynacker. Berchem was a pupil of Jan Baptist Weenix, and he painted figure details for Hobbema, Van Everdingen, and Ruisdael. He had important influence on Begeyn, Dujardin, De Hooch, and Ochtervelt.

Text: pp. 53, 73
Pictures: pp. 59, 74
His chief works are in Amsterdam, Berlin, Dresden, and Leningrad.

Berckheyde, Gerrit Adriaensz.
Haarlem 1638–1698

This distinguished architectural painter learned much from his elder brother, Job Adriaensz. Berckheyde. Influenced by his fellow city dweller, Pieter Saenredam, he painted and sketched many scenes of Dutch cities. They are characterized by straight lines, spareness, and orderliness.

Text: pp. 56–57
Pictures: pp. 62, 63
His chief works are in Amsterdam, The Hague, London, Brussels, and Vienna.

Berckheyde, Job Adriaensz.
Haarlem 1630–1693

Like his brother Gerrit, he lived and worked mainly in his home city as an architectural painter. He also depicted many churches, squares, and street scenes in neighboring cities, but he added spice to his scenes by using many human figures.

Text: pp. 57–58
Pictures: pp. 66, 71
His chief works are in Amsterdam, Dessau, Dresden, Leningrad, The Hague, Frankfurt, and Rotterdam.

Beyeren, Abraham van
The Hague *ca.* 1620–1690 Overschie

He was one of the most distinguished specialists in still-life painting. In his works, fish, fruit, flowers, and curios were decoratively combined, with only a casual allusion to the vanitas theme of perishability and of the transitory nature of existence.

Text: p. 110
Picture: p. 114
His chief works are in Amsterdam, The Hague, and Rotterdam.

Bloemaert, Abraham
Gorinchem 1566–1651 Utrecht

This versatile painter of the Utrecht school came under the influence of Caravaggio and the Romanists. He in turn influenced his pupils, Both, Cuyp, Honthorst, Terbrugghen, and Weenix.

Picture: p. 21

His chief works are in Copenhagen, Vienna, Munich, Brussels, The Hague, Berlin, and Amsterdam.

Bol, Ferdinand
Dordrecht 1616–1680 Amsterdam

Bol began in Amsterdam as a pupil of Rembrandt, and he excelled in mythological and Biblical themes. He soon became more popular as a portrait painter than his master, because he knew how to give his subjects an air of importance.

His chief works are in the Rijksmuseum in Amsterdam, and in Dresden and Leningrad.

Brouwer, Adriaen
Oudenarde ca. 1605–1638 Antwerp

The genre painting and peasant characterizations of Brouwer evoke the Flemish delight in lively, graphic painting. Brouwer worked in Amsterdam and Haarlem, where he joined the coterie of Frans Hals. The peasant scenes of Pieter Bruegel set the stage for Brouwer's painting, which in turn influenced the work of Teniers the Younger.

Text: pp. 10, 13, 16, 89, 90–93, 106
Pictures: pp. 98, 100
His chief works are in Dresden, Brussels, Frankfurt, Amsterdam, Madrid, London, Berlin, and Munich.

Bruegel, Jan
Brussels 1568–1625 Antwerp

Son of Pieter Bruegel and also known as "Velvet" Bruegel. Besides his detailed still lifes of flowers, he painted many thumbnail landscapes in the Flemish style. His style was influenced by Coninxloo and Paulus Bril. A much-sought-after detail painter, he provided background detail for works of Rubens and others. His son, Jan the Younger, continued his tradition.

Text: pp. 109–110, 112
Pictures: pp. 57, 116
His chief works are in Madrid, The Hague, Milan, Munich, Dresden, Vienna, Stockholm, and Amsterdam.

Bruegel, Pieter
Hertogenbosch ca. 1520–1569 Brussels

Also known as "Peasant Bruegel," he was a leading figure among Dutch genre painters. His studies and travels took him as far as Italy. He is famous for his multifigured peasant scenes, moralistic themes, and terraced panoramas of seasonal landscapes. Combined in his paintings were many motifs that became independent subjects of study by later specialists. His evident gift for graphic drawing reveals his ties with such earlier prototypes as Van Eyck and Hieronymus Bosch. Bruegel worked up countless patterns for engravings. Altogether, about 40 paintings, 100 sketches, and 300 engravings by him are known to us.

Text: pp. 16, 25, 27, 28, 33, 46, 48, 54, 60, 74, 89, 90, 91, 95
Pictures: pp. 14, 15, 17, 18, 19
His chief works are in Vienna, Naples, Paris, Berlin, and Prague.

Buytewech, Willem
Rotterdam ca. 1591–1624

Born in Rotterdam, he did most of his painting in Haarlem and belonged to the coterie of Frans Hals. He liked best to depict people drinking and making merry, and he painted elongated, elegantly garbed human figures. Buytewech was also an excellent etcher.

Text: p. 23
His chief works are in Amsterdam, Rotterdam, and Berlin.

Capelle, Jan van de
Amsterdam 1624–1679

He was an outstanding specialist in marine painting. Besides his delicate atmospheric studies of estuaries and calm seacoasts, he also painted winter scenes.

His chief works are in Berlin, Vienna, Amsterdam, London, and The Hague.

Claesz, Pieter
Burgsteinfurt 1597–1661 Haarlem

In Haarlem, he specialized in still lifes, in which simple objects and vessels are artfully combined on a table, with modest browns and grays providing the coloring. The allusion to the vanitas theme of the transitory nature of earthly joy is clear and unmistakable.

His chief works are in Kassel, The Hague, Budapest, and Amsterdam.

Coninxloo, Gillis van
Antwerp 1544–1607 Amsterdam

For religious reasons, this Flemish landscape painter emigrated to Frankenthal, Germany, in 1585, and lived there until 1595. He founded the Frankenthal school of painting, and his vivid woodland landscapes influenced many painters, including Bril, Elsheimer, and Ruisdael. Coninxloo spent his last years in Amsterdam.

Text: pp. 27–28
His chief works are in Vaduz and Dresden.

Cuyp, Aelbert
Dordrecht 1620–1691

As the leading figure of the Dordrecht school, he painted many landscapes and city scenes. He also painted seascapes, church pieces, still lifes, and scenes of animals and men. His style derives from Jan van Goyen. His later Southern landscapes are bathed in a golden light.

Text: pp. 10, 53
Pictures: pp. 22, 42

His chief works are in Amsterdam, Leningrad, Budapest, London, Frankfurt, Berlin, Rotterdam, Paris, and The Hague.

Cuyp, Benjamin
Dordrecht 1612–1652

Benjamin Cuyp was Jacob's step-brother. He painted sketchlike depictions of peasant life and action scenes, in the manner of Adriaen van Ostade.

His chief works are in Munich, Kassel, and Dessau.

Cuyp, Jacob Gerritsz.
Dordrecht 1594–ca. 1651

Jacob Cuyp, whose son Aelbert is better known, carried on the tradition of Abraham Bloemaert and painted peaceful, unassuming portraits, animal scenes, and story pieces.

Text: p. 107
Picture: p. 103
His chief works are in the Rijksmuseum in Amsterdam and in Cologne.

Dou, Gerard
Leyden 1613–1675

An important genre and portrait painter, his early work reveals the influence of his master, Rembrandt. He soon turned into a pedantic painter of museum pieces, placing the highest value on faithful reproduction of reality and its details. This painstaking attention to precise detail found many admirers and imitators, including Frans van Mieris, Gabriel Metsu, Pieter van Slingeland, Godfried Schalcken, and Quiringh van Brekelenkam.

Text: pp. 76–77, 106
His chief works are in Amsterdam, The Hague, Paris, Munich, Dresden, Florence, Leningrad, Hanover, Schwerin, Vienna, and London.

Eertvelt, Andries van
Antwerp 1590–1652

The sea scenes of this Flemish marine painter reveal his stylistic dependence on Pieter Bruegel. A picture of this early period depicts a sea voyage as a fantastic adventure. Like tiny toys, the ships are tossed on the bottle-green waves.

Text: p. 48
Picture: p. 49
His chief works are in Antwerp, Brussels, Amsterdam, Schwerin, and Düsseldorf.

Elsheimer, Adam
Frankfurt 1578–1610 Rome

This German painter and etcher did not belong to the Dutch school, but he had great influence on it. Early in his life, he went to Venice and Rome, where he came into close contact with other painters from the countries of Northern Europe. He became friends with Rubens, Lastman, and Bril, and his typically small-scale landscapes with impressive lighting effects influenced Rembrandt.

His chief works are in Berlin, Dresden, Frankfurt, Munich, and Prague.

Everdingen, Allaert van
Alkmaar 1621–1675 Amsterdam

This gifted pupil of Roelant Savery traveled to Norway and brought back many landscape sketches for his paintings. His melancholy scenes of the barren Scandanavian countryside influenced Jacob van Ruisdael, while his stormy sea scenes were imitated by Ludolf Backhuysen.

His chief works are in Amsterdam, Dresden, Vienna, Munich, and Braunschweig.

Fabritius, Barent
Middenbeemster 1624–1673 Amsterdam

His artistic beginnings were influenced by his elder brother Carel Fabritius and also by Rembrandt. In addition, he has stylistic ties with Nicolaes Maes. With his portraits of Biblical, mythical, and historical themes, he is a direct forerunner of Jan Vermeer.

His chief works are in Braunschweig, Turin, Kassel, Copenhagen, Aachen, Stockholm, Frankfurt, London, and Rotterdam.

Fabritius, Carel
Middenbeemster 1622–1654 Delft

Carel Fabritius, Rembrandt's most gifted pupil, painted striking genre scenes and self-portraits. Vermeer learned much from this important painter, whose life was cut short by the explosion of a powder magazine.

Text: pp. 56, 73, 143
His chief works are in Schwerin, Munich, Rotterdam, London, The Hague, Innsbruck, and Amsterdam.

Flinck, Govaert
Kleve 1615–1660 Amsterdam

This versatile pupil of Rembrandt excelled in painting portraits and mythological and Biblical themes. Around the middle of the century, he began accommodating himself to the changing tastes of the time along the lines of the successful painter Bartholomeus van der Helst.

Text: p. 79
His chief works are in Amsterdam, Munich, Berlin, Paris, Dresden, and Vienna.

Gelder, Aert de
Dordrecht 1645–1727

This curious master from Dordrecht took up the stylistic pattern of Rembrandt's later work. He continued Rembrandt's style of applying paint thickly, but he lacked the same power of expression. His work served as an important pattern for Rembrandt's imitators in the eighteenth century.

His chief works are in Dresden, Amsterdam, The Hague, Rotterdam, Dordrecht, Brussels, Copenhagen, Frankfurt, Munich, Hanover, Leningrad, Richmond, and Chicago.

Gheyn, Jacob (Jacques) de
Antwerp 1565–1629 The Hague

This artist did extensive work as a sketcher and etcher; his paintings are of lesser importance. Around 1585, he came to Haarlem as an apprentice of the influential engraver Hendrick Goltzius. In 1591, he set up his own shop in Amsterdam, and three years later he moved to The Hague, where he remained until his death. His precision prints of animal and plant life found many imitators in the seventeenth century and had an important influence on natural-science illustrations.

Picture: p. 109

His chief works are in the Rijksmuseum and National Print Collection in Amsterdam, in the Graphic Archives of Berlin and Munich, and in various private collections.

Goltzius, Hendrick
Venlo 1558–1617 Haarlem

This versatile painter was especially influential as an engraver, sketcher, and etcher. Around 1590, he studied in Rome and came under the influence of the Romanists. Together with Cornelis Cornelisz., he founded the Haarlem Academy, which had great influence on Dutch painters in the transitional period around 1600. The large-sized human figures of Goltzius are highly animated; their restless motion reveals their ties with the Mannerist style of the late sixteenth century.

His chief works are in Amsterdam, Rotterdam, and Munich; his graphics are in numerous collections.

Goyen, Jan van
Leyden 1596–1656 The Hague

After being trained by Esaias van de Velde in Haarlem, Van Goyen returned to his home city of Leyden. In his early period, this well-known landscape painter and sketcher remained under the stylistic influence of his teacher. Like Van de Velde, he painted scenes filled with people. After 1630, an impressive simplification in Van Goyen's work took place, and we find many impressive scenes of peaceful dunes. In his later period, softened tones of yellow, green, and brown predominate. Especially praiseworthy is his use of lighting, which contributes greatly to the over-all effect of the picture. Nicolaes Berchem and Jan Steen were his pupils, and there are close ties with Salomon van Ruysdael. Besides Aelbert Cuyp, many other landscapists followed the example of Van Goyen. More than 1,000 paintings have been attributed to him, but this figure is exaggerated.

Text: pp. 13, 28, 33–34, 45, 95, 112, 153
Pictures: pp. 26, 30, 40

His chief works are in Amsterdam, Dresden, Kassel, Basel, and in many other museums and private collections.

Mechlin ca. 1580–1666 Haarlem

A leading master of Dutch painting, he is closely identified with Haarlem. He is one of the greatest portrait painters of all time. A pupil of Karel van Mander (painter and author of a well-known biography of painters), Hals soon broke away from the Italian style and the academic tradition of Haarlem. From 1616 to 1627, his bold temperament seems to have found clear expression in his portraits of the civic guards. The carefree coloring of his work eventually gave way to the grandiose, somber portraits of his later period. The Impressionists regarded Hals as their spiritual forefather.

Text: pp. 10, 11, 12, 13, 56, 90, 93, 105, 106, 107, 126–41, 142–43, 156, 157, 169
Pictures: pp. 88, 126, 127, 129, 130, 131, 132, 133, 134, 135, 136, 139
His chief works are in Haarlem at the Frans Hals Museum, and in Amsterdam, Kassel, Berlin, Brussels, Paris, and Cologne.

Hals, Dirck
Haarlem 1591–1656

He was a genre painter and a brother of Frans Hals, who, along with Willem Buytewech and Esaias van de Velde, influenced him to paint scenes of happy merrymaking. Other lesser painters like Dirck Hals (Duyster, Codde, Duck, and Anthonie Palamedsz.), who belonged to the coterie of Frans Hals, took up the same type of genre painting. The scenes of elegantly clad merrymakers were readily salable.

His chief works are in Amsterdam, Vienna, Copenhagen, Budapest, Paris, Frankfurt, Cologne, London, and Bergamo.

Heda, Willem Claesz.
Haarlem 1594–1682

This specialist in still-life painting should not be confused with Pieter Claesz., whom he closely resembles in style and themes. His breakfast still lifes are clear and sober; gray-green and silver tones provide the coloring. The restricted use of color in the still lifes led people to designate them as "monochrome breakfast still lifes." This type of still life, which seems especially suitable to bring out the character of its materials (that is, silver, tin, glass, and the like), found many imitators. Among them was Heda's son, Gerrit Willemsz.

Text: pp. 13, 112, 121, 123, 124
Picture: p. 113
His chief works are in Amsterdam, The Hague, Aachen, Berlin, Budapest, Hamburg, Karlsruhe, Cologne, Leipzig, Munich, London, Dresden, and Rotterdam.

Helst, Bartholomeus van der
Haarlem 1613–1670 Amsterdam

Van der Helst was Rembrandt's most successful competitor in Amsterdam. With a talent for adaptation, he availed himself of the contributions of Rembrandt, Frans Hals, and Van Dyck. His brightly colored, large-sized, well-composed portraits proved to be decorative and pleasing, and he became a fashionable painter with many imitators. Posterity has not shared this high estimation of his work.

Picture: p. 141
His chief works are in Amsterdam, Karlsruhe, Florence, and Leningrad.

Hobbema, Meindert
Amsterdam 1638–1709

Hobbema was an important pupil of Jacob van Ruisdael, but he lacked his master's talent for dramatic display. His favorite themes are landscapes with windmills, sandy stretches, trees and avenues, isolated farms, and ruins. Human figures are unimportant. His careful use of lighting and his realistic harmonization of color tones made him a respected landscapist, although his later work shows traces of dull routine. His landscapes served as models for artists well into the nineteenth century.

Text: pp. 10, 13, 24, 45–46
Pictures: pp. 44, 55
His chief works are in Amsterdam, Antwerp, Paris, London, Frankfurt, and The Hague.

Hondecoeter, Melchior d'
Utrecht 1636–1695 Amsterdam

His father, Gysbert, was his first teacher. Melchior specialized in scenes of farmyard fowl and animal still life, marked by great artistic subtlety. His artistic training was carried further by his uncle, Jan Baptist Weenix, a renowned still-life painter. His grandfather was the lesser-known landscape painter Gillis Claesz. d'Hondecoeter, who painted in the manner of Roelant Savery.

Picture: p. 118
His chief works are in the Rijksmuseum in Amsterdam, and in Brussels and Leipzig.

Honthorst, Gerard van
Utrecht 1590–1656

A pupil of Abraham Bloemaert, Honthorst painted large-sized half-figures in the manner of Caravaggio; but his figures are more rustic and hearty than those of the better-known Terbrugghen. For a time, Honthorst's less gifted brother Willem worked with him.

Text: pp. 21, 76
His chief works are in Amsterdam, Dresden, Munich, and Utrecht.

Hooch, Pieter de
Rotterdam 1629–ca. 1684 Amsterdam

One of the Dutch masters in painting interiors. Two important stages during his long creative period were spent in The Hague and Delft. He began as a pupil of Nicolaes Berchem, getting inspiration from Carel Fabritius and Jan Vermeer. His popular paintings masterfully reflect the secure life of the Dutch burger during Holland's Golden Age.

Text: pp. 10, 12, 13, 60, 73–76, 77, 79, 107, 112, 142, 155
Pictures: pp. 65, 68, 82, 86
His chief works are in London, Amsterdam, Berlin, Paris, and Vienna.

Huysum, Jan van
Amsterdam 1682–1749

This important still-life painter was the son and pupil of Justus van Huysum (1659–1716). He is a typical representative of the later period, which came under the French influence and loved ostentatious display. The precise detail of his flowers, capturing the tiniest insect and beaded dewdrops, is unsurpassed.

Text: pp. 110–11
Pictures: pp. 117, 119
His chief works are in many galleries, including ones in London, Amsterdam, Paris, Munich, and Budapest.

Kalf, Willem
Amsterdam ca. 1622–1693

In his early period, this esteemed still-life painter also did thumbnail scenes of kitchens and storerooms. He is famous for his still-life paintings, which exquisitely frame costly vessels, exotic fruits, and other objects against a dark background.

Text: pp. 13, 121, 123
Picture: p. 120
His chief works are in many galleries, including ones in London, Amsterdam, Paris, and Berlin.

Koninck, Philips
Amsterdam 1619–1688

This well-known landscape artist was influenced by Hercules Seghers and Rembrandt but gained stature on his own right. His river scenes are usually viewed from a high vantage point. His paintings truly capture the melancholy nature of the shore, which is stretched out under trailing clouds and bathed in light and shadow. Dark colors predominate, mainly brownish green and ochre yellow. His sketches are also important; his Biblical scenes reveal his exact knowledge of Rembrandt's art.

Text: p. 45
Pictures: pp. 35, 37, 111, 124
His chief works are in Amsterdam, The Hague, Rotterdam, Berlin, Frankfurt, and Copenhagen.

Lastman, Pieter
Amsterdam 1583–1633

He may be regarded as Rembrandt's real teacher. His dramatic depiction of Biblical themes, rich in figures and gestures, served as a model for the work of his talented pupil's his early period.

Text: p. 157
His chief works are in Amsterdam, Rotterdam, The Hague, Augsburg, Braunschweig, Kassel, and Munich.

Lievens, Jan
Leyden 1607–1674 Amsterdam

Lievens was one of the painters in Rembrandt's circle. He was also a skilled sketcher and etcher, imitating Rembrandt's style and themes. Later, in Antwerp, he came under the influence of Ruben's style, and his own later style is large-scale and Baroque, like that of Bol, Flinck, or Maes. At first glance, the style is striking, but the impression does not remain long with the viewer.

Text: p. 80
His chief works are in Amsterdam, Braunschweig, Würzburg, and Leipzig.

Maes, Nicolaes
Dordrecht 1634–1693 Amsterdam

Maes began as Rembrandt's pupil around 1648. He returned to his home city for a while before, around 1673, setting up shop for good in Amsterdam. He began by painting Biblical scenes but soon moved away from his master and turned to pleasant, anecdotal genre scenes. He was also a popular portrait painter.

Text: pp. 79, 107
Pictures: pp. 81, 106, 154
His chief works are in London, Rotterdam, Dresden, Amsterdam, Berlin, Brussels, Munich, and in private collections.

Metsu, Gabriel
Leyden 1629–1667 Amsterdam

A younger contemporary of Rembrandt, he came nowhere near the lonely stature of the latter. His strong point was the painting of elegant genre scenes. Masters in Rembrandt's circle, including Gerard Dou and Nicolaes Maes, had an influence on his work. His careful reproduction of detail, his delicate execution, and his ability to please his subjects made him a very popular painter of glowing but commonplace genre scenes.

Text: pp. 10, 13, 76–79, 89, 142
Pictures: pp. 69, 83
His chief works are in Amsterdam, The Hague, Berlin, London, Paris, Dresden, Kassel, Munich, and in private collections.

Momper, Joos de
Antwerp 1564–1635

This landscape painter and sketcher typifies the original Flemish approach to landscape painting, a style spread by Flemish religious emigrés. Following the style of Pieter Bruegel, Momper mainly painted highly detailed scenes of craggy mountain peaks with diminutive human figures in the foreground. Fine and thinly coated, his paintings do not have the lively

originality of Bruegel's work; Nevertheless, they are pleasant and quaint museum pieces, depicting the craft of landscape painting and seasonal scenes. Frans de Momper of Antwerp continued this tradition.

Text: pp. 26, 27, 33
Pictures: pp. 20, 24
His chief works are in Munich, Braunschweig, Vaduz, and Pomerania.

Neer, Aert van der
Amsterdam 1603–1677

This landscape painter dealt mainly with moonlit landscapes and winter scenes. He gave his paintings a Romantic aura through the use of such lighting effects as sunsets and firelight. His son Eglon Hendrik van der Neer gained fame as a genre painter, in whose scenes the depicted elements seem deceptively true to life.

Text: p. 47
Picture: p. 31
His chief works are in Amsterdam, Antwerp, Kassel, Brussels, Berlin, Budapest, Frankfurt, Ghent, Hamburg, Leipzig, Leningrad, London, Vienna, and Braunschweig.

Netscher, Caspar
Heidelberg 1639–1684 The Hague

Netscher began as a promising pupil of Gerard Terborch but could not move away from the styles of the times. For a time, his style resembled that of Gabriel Metsu. Netscher ended by painting elegant miniature scenes in the French style.

His chief works are in Dresden, London, Munich, Amsterdam, Leningrad, Berlin, Kassel, and The Hague.

Nooms, Reinier (nicknamed "Zeeman," or "Seaman")
Amsterdam ca. 1623–ca. 1668

Influenced in his work by Willem van de Velde the Elder, this marine painter depicted small-scale scenes of Amsterdam and its port, as seen from the sea. He also did naval battles and Italian seacoasts. The atmosphere of his paintings is balanced, light, and misty.

Text: p. 48
Picture: p. 51
His chief works are in Amsterdam, Kassel, and Braunschweig.

Ochtervelt, Jacob
Rotterdam 1635–1710

This genre and portrait painter was a pupil of Nicolaes Berchem, then came under the influence of Pieter de Hooch. His most refined interior pieces show fine use of illumination and fine color harmony, but they are compositionally weak.

His chief works are in Amsterdam, Rotterdam, The Hague, Dresden, and Leningrad.

Ostade, Adriaen van
Haarlem 1610–1684

This painter and etcher was a pupil of Frans Hals and was also influenced by Adriaen Brouwer. Van Ostade's gay, dramatic paintings made him a leading interpreter of peasant life. The vivacious painter also did landscape figures for Pieter Saenredam, Jacob van Ruisdael, Jan Vermeer, and other colleagues. Approximately 1,000 paintings have been ascribed to him, although it is known that forgers and imitators were readily drawn to his work.

Text: pp. 53, 89, 93
Pictures: pp. 90, 92, 97
His chief works are in Paris, Munich, Kassel, London, Dresden, The Hague, Leningrad, Frankfurt, and Karlsruhe.

Ostade, Isaac van
Haarlem 1621–1649

The brother and pupil of Adriaen, he died at an early age. Isaac painted peasant scenes in yellow tones, as did his brother, and landscapes in the style of Wouwerman. Particularly impressive are his winter scenes, which are usually small in scale.

Text: pp. 10, 53
Pictures: pp. 43, 94
His chief works are in Amsterdam, Brussels, Berlin, Munich, Dresden, Leningrad, London, and Paris.

Porcellis, Jan
Ghent ca. 1584–1632 Leyden

This leading marine painter of the early period worked in Haarlem, Amsterdam, and Leyden. His sea scenes diverge from the traditional phantasmagoric approach, showing fine observation and atmosphere. The sea and sea voyages were no longer regarded with fear and trepidation. Jan van Goyen picked up this approach. Lesser talents, including Porcellis' son Julius and Jan Peeters, followed his lead.

Text: p. 48
Picture: p. 46
His chief works are in Amsterdam, Berlin, Darmstadt, Oldenburg, Munich, and Dessau.

Post, Frans
Leyden ca. 1612–1680 Haarlem

In 1637, this Dutch painter traveled to Brazil in the retinue of the governor, Johann Moritz von Nassau, and stayed there until 1644. He used his sketches and rough drafts of that period to paint his small-scale paintings of colonial scenes. They are characterized by groups of exotic figures and luminous coloring (blue and green). His brother Pieter (1608–69) was a lesser painter of battle scenes.

Text: p. 53
Picture: p. 50
His chief works are in Amsterdam, Liège, Leyden, Paris, London, Leningrad, Breslau, Mannheim, Karlsruhe, and Frankfurt.

Potter, Paulus
Enkhuizen 1625–1654 Amsterdam

Potter was the most important Dutch painter of animals in the seventeenth century. His subject matter was mainly grazing herds, cattle, sheep, goats, horses, and donkeys. His paintings are done with great care and fidelity to nature, and reveal placid landscapes in warm brownish-gold and light-green tones. He also executed countless sketches and etchings. His father was the lesser-known Pieter Potter. Paulus had many imitators in his special field well into the nineteenth century.

Text: pp. 9, 53
Pictures: pp. 39, 95
His chief works are in Amsterdam, The Hague, Munich, Dresden, Leningrad, and Kassel.

Rembrandt (Rembrandt Harmensz. van Rijn)
Leyden 1606–1669 Amsterdam

Son of a prosperous miller, he is the undisputed master of Dutch painting in the seventeenth century. He began as a pupil of Swanenburgh and Pieter Lastman. In 1631, he went to Amsterdam, and he soon gained renown. Adverse circumstances and his adherence to a style that the public did not understand brought him into great difficulties, and his later years were tragic ones. Although he had no pupils of equal genius, his paintings, sketches, and etchings exercised a powerful influence on knowledgeable contemporaries and or posteritiy.

Text: pp. 10, 12, 13, 16, 24, 27, 45, 76, 79–80, 91, 92, 105–6, 121, 127, 155, 156–76
Pictures: pp. 125, 151, 152, 159, 161, 162, 163, 164, 165, 166, 167, 168, 171, 172, 175, 176
His chief works are in many galleries and collections, including ones in Amsterdam, Berlin, Kassel, Munich, Dresden, Paris, Leningrad, Brussels, London, Braunschweig, Frankfurt, and Hanover.

Ruisdael, Jacob van
Haarlem ca. 1628–1682 Amsterdam

This great landscape painter, who came to Amsterdam around 1657, was first influenced by his uncle Salomon van Ruysdael. The landscape paintings of Esaias van de Velde also provided a prototype for Ruisdael's work, but Ruisdael soon acquired an independent style. His powerful landscapes, with thundering waterfalls, trees struck by lightning, and melancholy ruins, found many imitators and cast a spell over nineteenth-century Romantic poets and painters.

Text: pp. 12, 13, 24, 34, 35–36, 45, 47, 170
Pictures: pp. 27, 38, 41, 122
His chief works are in Amsterdam, Dresden, London, Berlin, Frankfurt, Glasgow, Leningrad, and Rotterdam.

Ruysch, Rachel
Amsterdam 1664–1750

A pupil of Willem van Aelst, he was a popular floral painter. His work is a late high point of Dutch still-life painting. Fruits or flowers are carefully arranged in exquisite compositions, and gleam like jewels against dark backgrounds. His chief works are in Dresden and in many galleries elsewhere.

Ruysdael, Salomon van
Haarlem *ca.* 1602–1670

Together with Jan van Goyen, Ruysdael was the founder of Dutch landscape painting. He is well known for his transparently painted seascapes, with boats, windmills, and sky, and for his village scenes. The color yellow is used predominantly in his early paintings, and the details are depicted in careful arrangements to suggest deep space or continuing space. The coloring is livelier in his later works. Salomon, uncle of the better-known Jacob van Ruisdael, differed from the latter in displaying greater reserve and delicacy. Hasty observers found this style somewhat tedious. Salomon had several less important imitators, including his son Jacob Salomonsz. Ruisdael, whose style lies somewhere in between that of his father and that of his more famous cousin.

Text: pp. 35–36, 45
Pictures: pp. 29, 34
His chief works are in Amsterdam, Vienna, Brussels, Munich, Budapest, and Hamburg.

Saenredam, Pieter
Assendelft 1597–1665 Haarlem

A contemporary of Frans Hals, he took an independent tack and devoted himself to architectural painting. His still-life, abstractive studies of church exteriors and interiors has won new attention in recent times, and the connection of his style with such moderns as Mondrian and Gropius is now recognized.

Text: pp. 123–24, 125
Picture: p. 115
His chief works are in Amsterdam, Haarlem, Rotterdam, Utrecht, Braunschweig, Budapest, Glasgow, Hamburg, Innsbruck, Kassel, London, and Turin.

Savery, Roelant
Courtrai 1576–1639 Utrecht

This Dutch master of the early period of the Golden Age painted small-scale woodland scenes containing many animals and flowers. He had stylistic ties with Jan Bruegel and Gillis van Coninxloo. Allaert van Everdingen was his pupil.

His chief works are in Amsterdam, Vienna, Munich, Dresden, and Dessau.

Seghers, Hercules
Haarlem *ca.* 1590–*ca.* 1638

This painter and etcher, who started out as a pupil of Gillis van Coninxloo, remains one of the most enigmatic of the Dutch painters; his life is shrouded in mystery. His landscapes, devoid of human figures, are peculiarly unquiet and turbulent. In them, crumbling rocks are piled up high, and sallow light casts an eerie shadow. His landscapes influenced Rembrandt and Philips Koninck, and they were rediscovered in the context of Surrealism. His landscape etchings, few of which survive, are very highly regarded.

Text: pp. 26–27, 33, 45, 169–70
Pictures: pp. 25, 32
His chief works are in Amsterdam, Berlin, Florence, The Hague, Paris, and Rotterdam.

Steen, Jan
Leyden 1626–1679

Jan Steen was an indefatigable painter of everyday Dutch life. He developed his work under the influence of Ostade, Brouwer, and Dirck Hals, living for a time in The Hague and Haarlem. Steen also assimilated ideas from Dou, Vermeer, de Hooch, and Frans van Mieris. His seemingly gay foreground scenes have a deeper meaning than might be noticed at first glance. They give expression to common-sense ideas and folk wisdom. Approximately 700 paintings of various types have been ascribed to this original painter, who had no pupils or imitators.

Text: pp. 13, 16, 58, 93–96, 107, 142
Pictures: pp. 67, 99, 101, 102
His chief works are in The Hague, Amsterdam, Kassel, London, Munich, Brussels, Paris, Vienna, Frankfurt, and Berlin.

Terborch, Gerard
Zwolle 1617–1681 Deventer

His name is also written as ter Borch. He is one of the most important Dutch genre and portrait painters. Like Willem Duyster, Pieter Codde, and Simon Kick, he began by painting mainly pictures of soldiers, but he turned his attention to depicting the upper burgher class. His figures radiate importance and superiority. Costly materials, such as silk and velvet, are reproduced in exquisite fashion. His careful style and remarkable use of colors influenced other great masters, such as Vermeer and Pieter de Hooch, and have delighted connoisseurs ever since.

Text: pp. 10, 13, 78, 89, 142
Pictures: pp. 72, 78, 87
His chief works are in Amsterdam, The Hague, London, Berlin, Dresden, Munich, Paris, Vienna, Kassel, Frankfurt, and Bremen.

Terbrugghen, Hendrick
Deventer 1588–1629 Utrecht

This pupil of Abraham Bloemaert is the best painter in the Utrecht school as influenced by Caravaggio and the Italian influence. Other painters influenced thus were Gerard van Honthorst, Jan van Bylert, and Dirck van Baburen. Terbrugghen is said to have been in Italy from 1604 to 1614, and he was more of a painter than his fellow Romanists.
Typical of the Utrecht school are large-scale half figures, brilliant colors, and surprising lighting effects.

Text: pp. 16, 21
Picture: p. 84
His chief works are in Utrecht, Kassel, Rome, Deventer, Augsburg, Gotha, Basel, Schwerin, Copenhagen, and London.

Velde, Adriaen van de
Amsterdam 1636–1672

This versatile landscapist was a pupil of Jan Wynants, and his brother was the marine painter, Willem van de Velde. He began with pictures of animal herds in the manner of Paulus Potter and went on to paint coastal scenes, winter scenes, and idyllic Southern landscapes. A skilled painter, he did figure details for Hobbema, Koninck, Ruisdael, Wynants, and others.

His chief works are in Amsterdam, London, Kassel, and Berlin.

Velde, Esaias van de
Amsterdam ca. 1591–1630 The Hague

This inventive landscapist mainly depicted seasonally changing scenes. The figure detail is skillfully done and has served as a model for the work of later painters. The same is true of his cavalry battles and pictures of horses. Jan van Goyen was influenced by his scenes of dunes.

Text: pp. 23, 32–33
His chief works are in Amsterdam, The Hague, Berlin, and Munich.

Velde, Willem van de, the Younger
Leyden 1633–1707 London

An important marine painter, he was the son of Willem van de Velde the Elder and a brother of Adriaen van de Velde. Simon de Vlieger was his teacher. His pictures of ships and naval battles reveal his exact knowledge of ship construction and the sea. He reproduced the atmosphere of the sea in magnificent style. The seafaring British greatly admired his work, which influenced the following generation of marine painters. In 1677, like his father before him, he became an English court painter.

Text: p. 48
Pictures: pp. 47, 52
His chief works are in Amsterdam, The Hague, London, and in many private collections in England.

Vermeer, Jan (Jan Vermeer van Delft)
Delft 1632–1675

Vermeer was one of the great Dutch masters of the seventeenth century. His pictures are notable for the tranquillity inherent in them, which gives them the aura of still-life scenes. The picture plane is often filled with a single figure who is occupied with some simple task (a kitchen maid, a person reading a letter, and the like). Complementary colors (especially blue and yellow) are beautifully harmonized. Vermeer's compositions are known also for their distinctive perspective, in which oversize details appear in the foreground. There are only forty of Vermeer's paintings that we are certain about, and none of his sketches remain. The long-neglected painter is now respected for his attention to detail, which gave the most commonplace objects an air of mystery.

Text: pp. 10, 12, 54–56, 58–60, 73, 75, 76, 77, 107, 112, 121, 124, 142–55, 156, 157
Pictures: book jacket; pp. 61, 70, 145, 146, 147, 148, 149, 150
His chief works are in The Hague, Dresden, Paris, Berlin, London, Amsterdam, Vienna, New York, Philadelphia, Washington, Frankfurt, and Edinburgh.

Verspronck, Johannes Cornelisz.
Haarlem 1597–1642

This pupil of Frans Hals was also influenced by Rembrandt's art. Although his execution lacks the lively energy of his great teacher, he was a keen-eyed portrait painter of his self-assured contemporaries in Haarlem.

Text: p. 107
Picture: p. 85
His chief works are in Amsterdam, Antwerp, Berlin, Budapest, Caen, Dessau, Frankfurt, Munich, and Paris.

Vlieger, Simon de
Rotterdam 1601–1653 Weesp

This leading master of Dutch marine painting depicted the varied moods of the sea in authentic fashion. His coastal scenes and etchings are also noteworthy. He was a pupil of Jan Porcellis and was influenced by Andries van Eertvelt and Hendrick Vroom. He was an important influence on his own pupils, Willem van de Velde the Younger and Jan van de Capelle.

Text: p. 48
His chief works are in Amsterdam, The Hague, London, Dresden, Kassel, Vienna, and Frankfurt.

Vroom, Hendrick
Haarlem 1566–1640

This marine painter of the early period produced sketchlike depictions of naval engagements and ships at sea, as seen from a high vantage point, that lack authentic atmosphere. The composition of Andries van Eertvelt is closely related. Also deserving of mention is Vroom's son, Cornelis, a capable landscape painter and a forerunner of Jacob van Ruisdael.

His chief works are in the Rijksmuseum in Amsterdam.

Weenix, Jan
Amsterdam 1640–1719

This versatile painter of the later period was the son and pupil of Jan Baptist Weenix (1621–63). He painted large-scale hunting still lifes, landscapes, and portraits. The decorative charm of his works cannot hide their lack of inner depth. From 1702 to 1712, he was a painter at the court of the Elector Palatine.

His chief works are in Amsterdam, Munich, Paris, Dresden, Vienna, and London.

Werff, Adriaen van der
Rotterdam 1659–1722

This academic painter of the later period was a pupil of Eglon van der Neer. His figures dress and move elegantly in the French manner. These overly elegant, bland paintings are one harbinger of a waning Golden Age. For a time, Adriaen lived in Düsseldorf as a Palatinate court painter. His brother Pieter van der Werff copied many of his works.

His chief works are in Munich, Amsterdam, Leningrad, and Dresden.

Witte, Emanuel de
Alkmaar 1617–1692 Amsterdam

Renowned for his church interiors, he also did landscapes, portraits, and pictures with religious and mythological themes. In contrast to the sketchlike architectural painting of Berckheyde and Saenredam, Witte used color for real artistic effect. His appealing interiors are suffused with warm, pleasant light.

Text: pp. 13, 124–25
Picture: p. 64
His chief works are in Rotterdam, Amsterdam, Brussels, Hamburg, Braunschweig, and London.

Wouwerman, Philips
Haarlem 1619–1668

This respected master specialized in pictures of horses and riders and in battle scenes. He was a pupil of his father, Paulus Wouwerman; his brothers, Jan and Pieter, were landscapists. Philips also painted figure details for Jacob van Ruisdael and Jan Wynants. His skillful paintings of horses found many imitators well into the eighteenth century, among them Johann Lingelbach and Dirck Stoop. More than 800 paintings have been attributed to him.

Text: p. 53
Picture: p. 104
His chief works are in Amsterdam, Dresden, Leningrad, Kassel, Paris, Munich, and The Hague.

LIST OF PLATES

189

On the jacket:

Jan Vermeer: *Man and Woman with Wine.*
Berlin, Gallery of Old Masters' Paintings.

Photo credits:

Hanfstaengl, Munich: p. 41; Marburg Photo, Lahn: pp. 18, 119; E. Meyer, Vienna: pp. 17, 72; Schuler-Verlag, Stuttgart: p. 81; H. Sibbelee, Nederhorst Den Berg: pp. 130, 131; World Press Photo, Amsterdam: p. 129; Westermann Photo (H. Buresch), Braunschweig: pp. 20, 29, 31, 32, 37, 49, 62, 65, 84, 103, 104, 113, 136, 149, 152, 161, 165. All other photographs come from the museums indicated above.